Basic Grammar in use

William R. Smalzer

with Raymond Murphy

CAMBRIDGE
UNIVERSITY PRESS

PUBLISHED BY THE PRESS SYNDICATE OF THE UNIVERSITY OF CAMBRIDGE
The Pitt Building, Trumpington Street, Cambridge, United Kingdom

CAMBRIDGE UNIVERSITY PRESS
The Edinburgh Building, Cambridge CB2 2RU, UK
40 West 20th Street, New York, NY 10011–4211, USA
477 Williamstown Road, Port Melbourne, VIC 3207, Australia
Ruiz de Alarcón 13, 28014 Madrid, Spain
Dock House, The Waterfront, Cape Town 8001, South Africa

http://www.cambridge.org

First published 2003

Printed in the United States of America

Typeface Sabon (Adobe®) System QuarkXPress®   [AH]

A catalog record for this book is available from the British Library
Library of Congress Cataloging in Publication data available

ISBN 0 521 79718 7 Workbook (with answers)
ISBN 0 521 79717 9 Workbook (without answers)
ISBN 0 521 62600 5 Student's Book (with answers)
ISBN 0 521 62599 8 Student's Book (without answers)

Illustrations: Randy Jones and Susann Ferris Jones
Art direction, book design, and layout services: Adventure House, NYC

Contents

To the Student v
To the Teacher vi

Present
Exercises 1 – 9 2
Review Exercises 10 – 11 12

Past
Exercises 12 – 16 14
Review Exercises 17 – 18 20

Present Perfect
Exercises 19 – 23 22
Review Exercise 24 27

Passive
Exercises 25 – 27 28
Review Exercise 28 31

Verb Forms
Exercises 29 – 30 32

Future
Exercises 31 – 32 34
Review Exercise 33 37

Modals, Imperatives, etc.
Exercises 34 – 41 38
Review Exercises 42 – 44 46

"There" and "It"
Exercises 45 – 47 50

Auxiliary Verbs
Exercises 48 – 52 54
Review Exercise 53 59

Questions
Exercises 54 – 59 60
Review Exercise 60 67

Reported Speech
    Exercise 61 68

"-ing" and "To"
    Exercises 62 – 65 70
    Review Exercises 66 – 67 74

"Go," "Get," "Do," "Make," and "Have"
    Exercises 68 – 71 76
    Review Exercises 72 – 73 80

Pronouns and Possessives
    Exercises 74 – 79 82
    Review Exercise 80 89

"A" and "The"
    Exercises 81 – 85 90
    Review Exercise 86 97

Determiners and Pronouns
    Exercises 87 – 96 98
    Review Exercise 97 109

Adjectives and Adverbs
    Exercises 98 – 104 110
    Review Exercises 105 – 107 117

Word Order
    Exercises 108 – 110 120
    Review Exercise 111 123

Prepositions
    Exercises 112 – 122 124
    Review Exercises 123 – 124 137

Two-Word Verbs
    Exercises 125 – 126 140

Conjunctions and Clauses
    Exercises 127 – 135 142
    Review Exercises 136 – 137 151

To the Student

Basic Grammar in Use Workbook provides you with practice in North American English, building on grammar points presented and practiced in the *Basic Grammar in Use* student's book. It offers additional exercises on difficult grammar points and a variety of exercises. The workbook will help you apply what you have learned in the student's book.

The workbook covers the same grammar points as the student's book. The types of exercises in the workbook are often different from those in the student's book, however. This way you can use what you have learned in a slightly different way. The exercises in this workbook will also help you understand how the grammar points in one unit of the student's book are related to the grammar in other units. You may be asked to use several different grammar structures in one exercise.

In general, workbook exercises will require you to read longer passages and write longer answers than the exercises in the student's book. In some exercises, you will rewrite whole sentences using different grammar structures but keeping the same meaning. In other exercises, you will read paragraphs and fill in blanks with correct forms. In review exercises, you will have the chance to write sentences using your own ideas.

Level

Like the student's book, the *Basic Grammar in Use Workbook* is intended for beginning and low-intermediate students. However, intermediate learners who have problems with grammar will also find the book useful.

How the workbook is organized

There are 137 exercises covering all 116 units in the student's book. One exercise in the workbook may cover the grammar in one, two, or three units in the student's book, however. Each exercise has a heading that tells which units of the student's book are covered in that exercise. Workbook exercises are grouped into sections, according to the sections in the student's book (see the Contents). At the end of most sections, there are review exercises.

How to use the workbook

Use the workbook after you have completed the corresponding units in the student's book. If you have trouble with the exercises on the right-hand pages of the student's book, review the explanations on the left-hand pages of those units. Then do the workbook exercises for those units.

To the Teacher

Basic Grammar in Use Workbook provides exercises to reinforce and extend the grammar lessons presented and practiced in the *Basic Grammar in Use* student's book. An exercise in the workbook often covers more than one unit in the student's book, in order to help students consolidate their knowledge of related grammar points. Thus, workbook exercises are often slightly more challenging than exercises in the student's book, in addition to having more varied formats.

The workbook covers all 116 units in the student's book. At the beginning of every workbook exercise is a heading that indicates the numbers and titles of the relevant units in the student's book. Intended to supplement the student's book, workbook exercises should be done after the relevant units in the student's book have been completed. Exercises in the workbook are organized into sections, corresponding to the sections in the Contents in the *Basic Grammar in Use* student's book. Review exercises can be found at the end of each section.

The book will be most useful for students at the beginning and low-intermediate levels. It will also be useful for intermediate students who need further practice on particular grammar points. Like the student's book, the workbook can be used by whole classes, by individual students needing extra help, or for independent study. Many of the exercises lend themselves better to writing than to oral work. These exercises may be done independently, or by students working together in the classroom.

This classroom edition of the *Basic Grammar in Use Workbook* contains no answer key. There is an edition with an answer key for teachers who prefer to have students check their own work or use the book on their own.

WORKBOOK

Basic Grammar in use

Am/is/are

Present

Write sentences about the people in the picture. Begin the sentences with *he, she, they,* or *it + is/are*. Then use the words in the box.

angry	~~cold~~	happy	hungry	interested in cars
thirsty	tired	very heavy	very tall	hot

1. (Andy) _He's cold._

2. (Sally) She _____ .

3. (Hannah and Jessica) They _____ .

4. (Ted) _____

5. (Mike and Carlos) _____

6. (Josh) _____

7. (Christina) _____

8. (Katie and Sarah) _____

9. (Teacher) _____

10. (Brandon's bookbag) _____

Write two sentences to answer each question: a positive sentence and a negative sentence.

1. Which is a big country? (Latvia, Russia)

   Russia is a big country.

   Latvia isn't a big country.

2. Which ones are warm countries? (Saudi Arabia, Finland, Poland, Brazil)

   Saudi Arabia and Brazil are warm countries.

   Finland and _____ .

3. Which of these are expensive? (tea, diamonds, a newspaper)

   _____

   _____

4. Which of these cities are in Canada? (Atlanta, Vancouver, Toronto)

   _____

   _____

5. Are you married or single?

   _____

   _____

6. Which of these cities are in South America? (Madrid, Santiago, Lima, Buenos Aires)

   _____

   _____

7. Which are necessary for a cake? (eggs, butter, pepper, sugar)

   _____

   _____

8. Are you and your family from Brazil or from another country?

   We _____ .

   _____

Am/is/are (Questions)

Write questions with the words in parentheses and *am*, *is*, or *are*. Use any other words that are necessary, and use question marks. Read the answers first.

Questions	Answers
1. (your parents) *Where are your parents?*	They're at home.
2. (you / cold) *Are you cold?*	No, I'm fine.
3. (your friend / from Russia)	No, she's from Poland.
4. (your parents)	They're fine, thanks.
5. (Linda's apartment)	It's on Third Street.
6. (tired)	No, I'm not.
7. (this postcard)	It's 25 cents.
8. (Julia's hair)	It's red this week.
9. (your teachers / nice)	Yes, I think they are.
10. (you)	I'm 29.
11. (angry with me)	Because you are always late!
12. (those people)	They're my aunt and uncle.
13. (their names)	Jeff and Alice Turner.
14. It looks cold outside. (right)	Yes, you're right. It is very cold.

UNIT
3

I am doing (Present Continuous)

Look at each picture. Use the words in parentheses to write two sentences in the present continuous: a positive sentence and a negative sentence.

1. A: (listen to the radio)

    Zack *isn't listening to the radio* .

    B: (watch TV)

    He *'s watching TV* .

2. A: (play soccer)

    Jessica _____ .

    B: (do her homework)

    She _____ .

3. A: (eat at home)

    The Millers _____ .

    B: (have dinner in a restaurant)

    They _____ .

4. A: (sit in the park)

    Mr. Jensen _____ .

    B: (work now)

    _____

5. A: (write a letter)

    She _____ .

    B: (study English)

    _____

6. A: (fix the car)

    Ms. Monroe _____ .

    B: (wash the car)

    _____

UNIT
4

Are you doing . . . ? (Present Continuous Questions)

A friend is visiting town and leaves a phone message. Write questions for your friend with the words in parentheses. (Note: Not all the questions will be in the present continuous.)

> Hi. This is Sam Chung. It's about 10 in the morning, and we are in town for a day. We're leaving tomorrow. I want to see you. Are you busy?
>
> Also, I need information on good places to visit in town. I'll call you again later today. Bye.

Questions for Sam

1. (why / leave / so soon) *Why are you leaving so soon?*

2. (where / stay) _____

3. (travel / with somebody) _____

4. (see / other friends here) _____

5. (how / enjoy / my town) _____

6. (how / get / around town) _____

7. (visit / famous places here) _____

8. (interested in art museums) _____

9. (where / now) _____

10. (what / do now) _____

I do, I work, I like, etc. (Simple Present)
I don't . . . (Negative Simple Present)

Use the words in parentheses, and write sentences that make sense with* the first sentence. Write positive or negative sentences as needed.

1. Mia isn't a good traveler.

    (like / different kinds of food) *She doesn't like different kinds of food.*

    (like / to sleep in her own bed) She *likes to sleep in her own bed* .

    (enjoy / new places) _____

    (know / other languages) _____

    (like / to take airplanes) _____

2. Andrew isn't in very good health*.

    (eat / healthy food) He _____ .

    (sleep / enough) _____

    (smoke / a lot) _____

3. Angela's and Paul's lives are hard.

    (make / a lot of money) They _____ .

    (live / in a very nice place) _____

    (have / boring jobs) _____

4. I have a lot of friends.

    (like to be with people) I _____ .

    (talk / about others behind their back*) _____

    (listen / to others' problems) _____

5. You are a very good boss.

    (listen / to your employees*) You _____ .

    (work / hard) _____

    (get / angry often) _____

    * make sense with: *to go together logically*
    * be in good health: *to be well*
    * talk about others behind their back: *to say bad things about others when they are not there*
    * employee: *someone who is paid to work for someone else*

UNIT
7

Do you . . . ? (Simple Present Questions)

You meet a young woman from Quebec City, Canada. Write questions to ask her. Use the words in parentheses in the right order. Add necessary words. (Look at the answers first.)

Your questions	**The woman's answers**
1. (like / Quebec) _Do you like Quebec?_	Yes, I like it a lot.
2. (snow / it / a lot / there / in the winter) Does _____ ?	Yes, it does. And it's usually very cold.
3. (do / there) What _____ ?	I am a French teacher.
4. (teach / French as a second language) _____	No, I teach French as a first language.
5. (children in Quebec / study / French) _____	Yes. Most of them do.
6. (people in Quebec / speak / French) _____	Not everyone does, but most people do.
7. (students / have / in your class) How _____ ?	I have 20 in one class, and 25 in the other one.
8. (many tourists / visit / Quebec City) _____	Yes, a lot visit in the summer.
9. (teach / in the summer) _____	No, I'm usually free in the summer.
10. (take / a vacation every year) _____	Yes, I try to.
11. (go / usually) _____	I travel to other parts of Canada. Sometimes I go to the United States or South America.

UNIT
8

I am doing and *I do* (Present Continuous and Simple Present)

A. Answer the questions about the pictures. Write full sentences or short answers as needed.

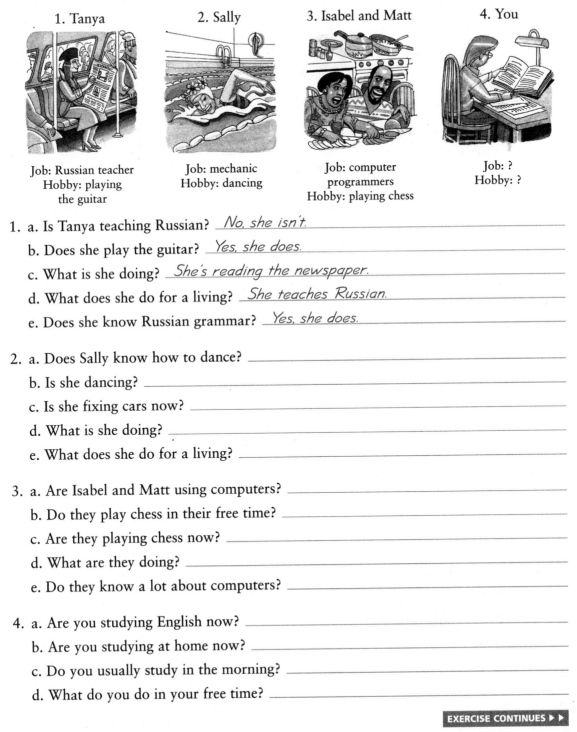

1. Tanya
2. Sally
3. Isabel and Matt
4. You

Job: Russian teacher
Hobby: playing
the guitar

Job: mechanic
Hobby: dancing

Job: computer
programmers
Hobby: playing chess

Job: ?
Hobby: ?

1. a. Is Tanya teaching Russian? *No, she isn't.*
   b. Does she play the guitar? *Yes, she does.*
   c. What is she doing? *She's reading the newspaper.*
   d. What does she do for a living? *She teaches Russian.*
   e. Does she know Russian grammar? *Yes, she does.*

2. a. Does Sally know how to dance? _____
   b. Is she dancing? _____
   c. Is she fixing cars now? _____
   d. What is she doing? _____
   e. What does she do for a living? _____

3. a. Are Isabel and Matt using computers? _____
   b. Do they play chess in their free time? _____
   c. Are they playing chess now? _____
   d. What are they doing? _____
   e. Do they know a lot about computers? _____

4. a. Are you studying English now? _____
   b. Are you studying at home now? _____
   c. Do you usually study in the morning? _____
   d. What do you do in your free time? _____

EXERCISE CONTINUES ▶ ▶

B. Write the questions that go with the answers. Use the words in parentheses.

1. Anne
2. Seth
3. Luke
4. Emily

Job: dentist
Hobby: running

Job: news reporter
Hobby: playing the
piano

Job: house husband*
Hobby: computer
games

Questions

1. a. (Anne / do) _What does Anne do (for a living)?_

   b. (fix teeth) _Is she fixing teeth?_

   c. (do in her free time) _What does she do in her free time?_

   d. (run) _Is she running?_

2. a. (Seth / do) _____

   b. (write / a story) _____

   c. (do) _____

   d. (sit) _____

   e. (use / a computer for work) _____

3. a. (Luke / cook) _____

   b. (cook) _____

   c. (play / computer games) _____

   d. (do) _____

4. a. (Emily / laugh) _____

   b. (eat) _____

   c. (speak / English) _____

   d. (look / happy) _____

Answers

She's a dentist.

Yes, she is.

She runs.

No, she isn't.

He's a reporter.

No, he isn't.

He's playing the piano.

At the piano.

Yes, he does.

Yes, he does.

Yes, he is.

Yes, he does

He's a house husband*.

Yes, she is.

No, she isn't.

No, she doesn't. She's too young.

Yes, she does.

* house husband: *a married man who works at home taking care of the house and children*

UNIT
9

I have . . . and I've got . . .

A. Use your own ideas to write sentences with the words in parentheses. Write about yourself, members of your family, or your friends. Use have/has or don't/doesn't have.

1. (a car) *I have a new car.* OR *I don't have a car.* OR *My friend has a new car.*

2. (a lot of friends) _____

3. (a part-time job) _____

4. (an earache) _____

5. (a lot of free time) _____

B. Use your own ideas to write sentences with the words in parentheses. Use have/has got or haven't/hasn't got.

1. (a car) *My father has got a car.* OR *I haven't got a car.*

2. (a passport) _____

3. (a lot of money) _____

4. (a lot of problems) _____

5. (a fast computer) _____

C. Complete the questions and answers. Use do, doesn't, don't, got, has, have, hasn't, or haven't.

Questions	Answers
1. Does this house *have* a big back yard?	Yes, it *does* . And the yard is full of trees.
2. _____ Amy got a cold?	No. She _____ got a cold. She has a sore back.
3. Do the Turners _____ a dog?	No, they _____ . But they have a cat.
4. Has your car _____ a big engine?	Yes. It _____ got a very big engine, and it uses a lot of gas.
5. _____ Kim have her own computer?	No, she _____ . She uses her brother's.
6. Have you _____ change for a dollar?	Sorry. I _____ got any change. Ask in the drugstore.

Read the story about a young college woman. Then complete the sentences with the simple present or present continuous of the verbs given.

Sara Mitchell is nineteen years old. She **1)** _goes_ (go) to college. She **2)** _is studying_ (study) music. She **3)** _____ (play) the violin, and she **4)** _____ (sing) beautifully. She **5)** _____ (study) Spanish, too. She **6)** _____ (love) music, but Spanish **7)** _____ (seem) very difficult to her. She often **8)** _____ (sing) in other languages in her music classes, but usually she **9)** _____ (not / understand) the meaning of the words. This year in school she **10)** _____ (learn) a different language for the first time. She **11)** _____ (need) to learn a lot of new words in Spanish, and she sometimes **12)** _____ (forget) the Spanish words in class and on tests.

Sara **13)** _____ (have) an apartment near the college with three roommates – Molly, Kate, and Alicia. Sara's roommates **14)** _____ (go) to the college too, and Sara **15)** _____ (like) them all a lot. They always **16)** _____ (do) things together. They often **17)** _____ (eat) dinner in the apartment together, and they usually **18)** _____ (go) to the movies together on Friday nights. But right now they **19)** _____ (not / think) about movies.

Right now Sara **20)** _____ (study) for a big Spanish exam. Sara usually **21)** _____ (not / do) well on Spanish exams, and she is very worried. Alicia **22)** _____ (speak) Spanish well, so she **23)** _____ (help) Sara study for the test. Molly and Kate **24)** _____ (make) dinner for her. Sara is very lucky to have such nice roommates, and she knows it!

EXERCISE 11

REVIEW

Present

Use your own ideas to write sentences with the words in parentheses. Use the simple present or present continuous.

1. (remember / my first day of school) *I remember my first day of school.*
   OR *My mother doesn't remember my first day of school.*

2. (listen / to music) *I'm listening to music right now.*

3. (do / this exercise / on the computer) _____

4. (play / the guitar) _____

5. (understand / English grammar) _____

6. (it / rain / right now) _____

7. (use / a computer / at work / very often) _____

8. (it / rain / a lot / here / in the summer) _____

9. (like / lazy people) _____

10. (send / e-mail / to my friends / every day) _____

11. (have got / plans for tonight) _____

12. (watch / TV / now) _____

Past

Was/were
Worked, got, went, etc. (Simple Past)
I didn't . . . Did you . . . ? **(Simple Past Negative and Questions)**

**A. Write two sentences about each picture: a positive one and a negative one.
Use the words in parentheses. Put the verb in the simple past.**

1. *A:* (be / late for school / yesterday)
   Lisa *wasn't late for school yesterday* .
   B: (get / to school / on time)
   She got to school on time.

2. *A:* (do / his homework / yesterday afternoon)
   Steve *didn't do his homework yesterday afternoon.* .
   B: (play / tennis with a friend)
   He _____

3. *A:* (be / tired / Friday night)
   Andrew and Megan _____ .
   B: (go / to the gym)
   They _____ .

4. *A:* (bring / her lunch to work / yesterday)
   Jessica _____ .
   B: (eat / in a restaurant with her friends)
   _____

5. *A:* (be / late for work / this morning)
   Martin _____ .
   B: (get up / at 7:30)
   _____

6. *A:* (drive / to Miami / last week)
   Nicholas and Rosa _____ .
   B: (fly / first class)
   _____

EXERCISE CONTINUES ▶ ▶

B. Now write questions about the people in Part A. Use the words in parentheses. Add any necessary words. Read the answers first.

Questions	Answers
1. (Lisa / get / to school) *What time did Lisa get to school?*	At 8:25.
2. (Steve / do / his homework) When _____ ?	After dinner.
3. (Andrew and Megan / be / tired / last night) Why _____ ?	Because they have difficult jobs.
4. (Jessica's friends / eat) _____	At a Chinese restaurant.
5. (Martin / get up / late / this morning) _____	Because he went to bed late last night.
6. (Nicholas and Rosa / fly / to Miami) _____	Last week.

Was/were
Worked, got, went, etc. (Simple Past)
I didn't . . . Did you . . . ? (Simple Past Negative and Questions)

Complete the paragraphs about getting a driver's license. Use the verbs in the boxes in the simple past.

be	drive	move	~~need~~	want

I **1)** *needed* a car when I **2)** _____ from Japan to Los Angeles.
After all, public transportation isn't very good in Los Angeles. A person in that city
needs a car to get from home to work and school. At first, my friends in Los Angeles
3) _____ me to work and school. They **4)** _____ nice to me,
but I **5)** _____ to get a car too. With a car, people have more freedom.
First, I had to get a driver's license.

arrive	be	be	bring	read	learn

I **6)** _____ the *California Driver Handbook* to find out about driving in
California. I **7)** _____ how to make a left turn correctly and how fast to
drive near a school and on a highway*. The rules **8)** _____ new and difficult for
me. The day of my test, a friend **9)** _____ me to the place for the driving
test in his car. I **10)** _____ very nervous when I **11)** _____ there.

be	be	make	pass	take

I **12)** _____ two driving tests: a written one and a road test.
Fortunately, I **13)** _____ both tests. I **14)** _____ surprised
because I think I **15)** _____ a mistake during the road test. But the examiner*
16) _____ satisfied* with my driving. I am happy to have my own driver's license.
Now all I need is a car!

* highway: *a wide road where cars can drive fast*
* examiner: *a person who gives a test*
* satisfied: *happy or pleased*

EXERCISE 14

I was doing (Past Continuous)

Complete the conversations with the words in parentheses. Use the past continuous (*was/were* + *-ing*).

1. *A:* _What were you doing_____ (What / you / do) at nine last night?

   B: _We were visiting_____ (we / visit) my aunt in the hospital. Why?

   A: I drove by your house, but no one was home.

2. *A:* _____ (you / sleep) at midnight last night?

   B: Yes, I go to bed around 11. Why?

   A: There was a fire at the factory near your house. Didn't you hear the fire trucks?

   B: I think I remember hearing some noise, but I thought _____ (I / dream).

3. *A:* I saw you yesterday. I waved at you, but you didn't see me.

   B: _____ (What / I / do?)

   A: _____ (you / drive) down First Avenue about 10 A.M.

   B: Oh, _____ (I / come) from the dentist. I didn't notice you.

   I guess _____ (I / concentrate*) on driving.

4. *A:* Why _____ (Sue / cry) a little while ago?
   What happened?

   B: _____ (she / not / cry). _____ (she / laugh).

   _____ (some friends / tell) jokes, and she couldn't
   stop laughing.

5. *A:* That was Ellie Bates who _____ (you / talk) to before,
   wasn't it? I didn't know you know her. How did you meet her?

   B: I met her when _____ (I / live) in Washington.

   _____ (she and my wife / work) in the same office.

* concentrate: *to keep your attention on something*

UNIT
14

I was doing and *I did* (Past Continuous and Simple Past)

Complete the conversations with the words in parentheses. Use the simple past or the past continuous.

1. A: _Did you go out for lunch today?_ (you / go out / for lunch today?)

   B: No, I was in my office at lunchtime. I _was waiting for an important phone call_ (wait / for an important phone call).

2. A: _____ (you / go / out last night?)

   B: No. It _____ (rain).

   We _____ (not / want / to get wet).

3. A: I'm sorry I'm late. I _____ (miss) the train.

   It _____ (leave) the station when I _____ (arrive) at the track.

   B: That's OK. I _____ (finish) my homework while I _____ (sit) here.

4. A: Were you at home at 7 last night? I _____ (call) you, but no one _____ (answer).

   B: I _____ (watch) some music videos at that time. There was a lot of noise, so I guess I _____ (not / hear) the phone ring.

5. A: How _____ (Tim / hurt / himself)?

   B: He _____ (play / soccer in the park), and he _____ (fall).

6. A: What _____ (you / do) after the accident _____ (happen)?

   B: I _____ (call / the police) on my cell phone.

7. A: What _____ (you / do) when the electricity _____ (go out)?

   B: I _____ (cook / dinner).

8. A: _____ (you / see / John at work today?)

   B: Yes, but we _____ (not / have / time to talk).

I used to . . .

Look at the pictures. They show the people *now*. Use the words in parentheses and *but* to write a sentence about now and the past.

1. (lawyer /musician)

   Ed Simms *is a lawyer now, but he used to be a musician* .

2. (go to bed early / stay up late)

   Marge and Stan _____ now,

   but they _____ .

3. (own* a restaurant / be a professional baseball player)

   Michael _____ now,

   but _____ .

4. (go out a lot / stay home every night)

   Rachel and her husband _____ now,

   _____ .

5. (be bald / have long hair)

   Art _____

   _____ .

6. (drive a car / ride a bike)

   Carol _____

   _____ .

7. (eat at home / eat in restaurants)

   Felix _____

   _____ .

8. (be a very big city / be a small place)

   My hometown _____

   _____ .

* own: *to have something, often a house or a business*

The police are investigating a break-in* in a neighborhood. They are asking people questions. Complete the conversation with the simple past or past continuous of the verbs in parentheses.

Police officer: **1)** *Were you* _____ (you / be) at home between four and five today?

Neighbor: No, I **2)** _____ (be) at work. Why, officer?

Police officer: Someone **3)** _____ (break) into the Brocks' house this afternoon.

4) _____ (anyone else / be) at your house between four and five?

Neighbor: My son **5)** _____ (not / go) to class this afternoon. He's sick. But I don't think he **6)** _____ (see) anything. I'm sure he **7)** _____ (sleep).

Police officer: What time **8)** _____ (you / come) home from work?

Neighbor: At 5:30, as usual.

Police officer: **9)** _____ (you / see) anything unusual at that time?

Neighbor: Let me think. Now that you ask, I think the Brocks' garage door **10)** _____ (be) open. And their dog **11)** _____ (sit) in the front yard. That was unusual, I guess, but I **12)** _____ (not / think) anything of it at the time. **13)** _____ (anyone / see) the thieves?

Police officer: No, it seems many of the neighbors **14)** _____ (prepare) dinner, and others **15)** _____ (watch) the news on TV.

Neighbor: **16)** _____ (the thieves / take) anything?

Police officer: No, it seems that they **17)** _____ (not / know) there was a dog in the house. I think that they **18)** _____ (look) for money or jewelry and they were surprised by the dog.

Neighbor: I'm surprised that thieves **19)** _____ (choose) the Brocks' house. The Brocks are retired*, so they are almost always at home.

Police officer: They **20)** _____ (take) some friends to the airport. When they **21)** _____ (get) home around six, they **22)** _____ (call) the police.

Neighbor: Is there anything else I can do for you?

Police officer: No. Thanks, you have been very helpful.

* a break-in: *entering a house by breaking a window or a door to steal things*
* retired: *not working anymore, usually because of age*

Use your own ideas to write sentences with the words in parentheses. Use the simple past, the past continuous, or _used to_. Write positive and negative sentences.

1. (eat / dinner at 7 P.M. last night) _My family ate dinner at 7 P.M. last night._
   (= We sat down and began to eat at 7.)
   OR _My family was eating dinner at 7 P.M. last night._
   (= We started before 7 and the meal was in progress at 7.)

2. (go / to bed early / when / be / a child) _I used to go to bed early when I was a child._

3. (sleep / at 2:30 in the morning) _____

4. (drive / to work last week) _____

5. (go / to the movies yesterday) _____

6. (play / soccer / when / be / a child) _____

7. (stay / home last night) _____

8. (study / a lot / when / be / in secondary school) _____

9. (have / an accident when / drive / home the other night) _____

10. (talk / on the phone at six this morning) _____

11. (cry / when / hear / the bad news) _____

EXERCISE 19

Have you ever . . . ? (Present Perfect)

A. Look at the pictures. Use your own ideas to write sentences in the present perfect with the words in parentheses.

1.   2.   3.   4.

5.   6.   7.   8.

1. (ride a motorcycle) *I've never ridden a motorcycle.* OR *I've ridden a motorcycle once.*

2. (sing in public) _____

3. (drive a truck) _____

4. (eat alone at a restaurant) _____

5. (change a flat tire) _____

6. (cook dinner for ten people) _____

7. (be to Paris) _____

8. (break an arm) _____

B. Now write questions with *ever*. Use the present perfect and the same words in parentheses as in Part A.

1. *Have you ever ridden a motorcycle?*   5. _____

2. Have you ever _____ ?   6. _____

3. _____   7. _____

4. _____   8. _____

Write questions with *How long has/have* to complete the conversations. Use the present perfect or the present perfect continuous. Look at A's first statement as a clue for which form of the verb to use.

1. *A:* I'm working in a bank now.

   B: How nice. *How long have you been working* there?

   A: For three months.

2. *A:* My father is in Australia on business.

   B: Really? *How long has he been* there?

   A: Since last Monday.

3. *A:* Eric is waiting for a phone call from his uncle.

   B: He is? How long _____ the phone call?

   A: All day.

4. *A:* Did you know that Marcia is a Spanish teacher now?

   B: No. _____ a teacher?

   A: She just started.

5. *A:* My parents are traveling around the country.

   B: Really? _____

   A: For the past two months.

6. *A:* I'm studying Japanese for my trip to Tokyo.

   B: Great. _____ it?

   A: Just a few weeks – this is my first course.

7. *A:* I have a terrible headache.

   B: You poor thing! _____ it?

   A: Since I woke up this morning.

8. *A:* Some good friends of mine live in Hawaii.

   B: Lucky them! _____ there?

   A: They just moved there.

EXERCISE 21

For, since, and *ago*

Answer the questions. Use the words in parentheses and *for, since,* or *ago*.

Questions	Answers
1. Does Martin still live in Seattle?	(go to Africa / a year)
	No, *he went to Africa a year ago* .
2. Does Martin still live in Seattle?	(be in Africa / a year)
	No, *he has been in Africa for a year* .
3. Does Martin still live in Seattle?	(be in Africa / last year)
	No, *he has been in Africa since last year* .
4. Have you had breakfast yet?	(have it / a half hour)
	Yes, I _____ .
5. Is it still raining?	(rain / a long time)
	Yes, it _____ .
6. Do the Lees still live in Philadelphia?	(move to Boston / six months)
	No, they _____ .
7. Is your uncle still in the hospital?	(be there / almost three weeks)
	Yes, _____ .
8. Have you always had dark hair?	(have dark hair / I was little)
	Yes, _____ .
9. Is your headache gone?	(take some aspirin / an hour)
	Yes, _____ .
10. Have your parents been living in Florida long?	(live there / 1982)
	Yes, _____ .
11. Is your son a doctor yet?	(study medicine / three years)
	No, but _____ .
12. Did you meet your husband at work?	(know each other / we were in high school)
	No, _____ .

UNITS
19-20

I have done and *I did* (Present Perfect and Simple Past)
Just, already, and *yet* (Present Perfect and Simple Past)

A. Complete the conversations with the words in parentheses and any other necessary words. Use the present perfect.

1. *A:* Is Andrew Martinez in college?

   B: No, he *hasn't finished high school yet* (finish / high school / yet).

2. *A:* Would you like some coffee?

   B: No thanks. *I've just had some lemonade* (just / have / some lemonade).

3. *A:* Are you going to Australia on vacation?

   B: No, we _____ (already / be / there).

4. *A:* I think you should read this book. It's great.

   B: Thanks, but _____ (already / read / it).

5. *A:* _____ (you / see / the boss / yet?)

   B: No, he's been busy all morning.

6. *A:* Are you going to the movies with us?

   B: No, I'm waiting for a phone call, and I _____ (get / it / yet).

7. *A:* _____ (go / to the post office / yet?)

   B: Yeah, why? Do you need something?

B. Complete the conversations with the words in parentheses and any other necessary words. Use the simple past.

1. *A:* Is Carl watching TV?

   B: No, he *didn't finish his homework yet* (finish / his homework).

2. *A:* *(on the phone)* You sound strange. What's wrong?

   B: Nothing. I _____ (just / get up).

3. *A:* You need to speak to the boss.

   B: I _____ (already / speak / to her).

4. *A:* I don't think Jeremy knows his mother's in the hospital.

   B: Maybe his father _____ (tell / him / yet).

I've lost my key.
I lost my key last week. (Present Perfect and Simple Past)

Use the words in parentheses to write sentences in the simple past or the present perfect. Some are questions.

1. (my cousin / visit / many countries since he became a pilot) _My cousin has visited_ _many countries since he became a pilot._

2. (your brother / go / to China last year?) _Did your brother go to China last year?_

3. (my friends / never / eat / Ethiopian food) _____

4. (what time / you / wake up / this morning?) _____

5. (my friend / have / the same job since college) _____

6. (you / ever / be / to Norway?) _____

7. (you / eat / a lot of good food / on your last vacation?) _____

8. (I / not / meet / your parents / until two years ago) _____

9. (you / lose / your wallet at home or at work?) _____

10. (Dean's father / start / his new job / last week) _____

11. (you / ever / stay / at a hotel on the beach?) _____

12. (Janeen / know / her best friend since elementary school) _____

Use your own ideas to write sentences with the words in parentheses. Use the simple present, simple past, or present perfect.

1. (live / in) *I live in Istanbul.* OR *I've lived in Istanbul since I was born.*
   OR *I didn't live in Istanbul from 1999 to 2001.*
   _____

2. (know / my best friend / since) _____

3. (have / the same hairstyle / for) _____

4. (buy / something expensive / ago) _____

5. (never / see / before) _____

6. (be / Australia) _____

7. (life / change / a lot) _____

8. (not / do / yet) _____

9. (take / last year) _____

10. (be / sick / a few days) _____

11. (work / for the same company / a long time) _____

12. (just / remember) _____

13. (go / to bed / last night) _____

14. (live / in many places) _____

15. (already / eat) _____

UNIT
22

Passive

Is done and *was done* (Passive)

Use the words in parentheses to write sentences in the passive (present or past). Some are questions.

1. *A:* This city is very crowded.

   B: (more houses / build / every year) Yes. <u>*More houses are built every year.*</u>

2. *A:* Did you do well on your exam?

   B: (we / not / give / enough time) No. <u>*We weren't given enough time.*</u>

3. *A:* Why didn't you receive your phone bills?

   B: (they / sent / to my old address) _____

4. This plant is very rare. (it / find / in only a few places) _____

   _____

5. *A:* Is soccer popular in Canada?

   B: (it / not / play much / twenty years ago) _____

   _____ However, it is very popular now.

6. (oil / not / import / by Venezuela) _____
   The country produces a lot of oil and exports it.

7. Someone broke into your house? (anything / steal?) _____

8. *A:* (anyone / injure / in the accident?) _____

   B: Yes, unfortunately. (two people / take / to the hospital) _____

   _____

9. *A:* (how many people / need / to make a basketball team?) _____

   _____

   B: There are five on each team.

10. *A:* What are those flowers?

    B: (they / call / "daffodils") _____

11. *A:* (when / this package / deliver / here?) _____

    B: I don't know for sure. Sometime this morning, I think.

Put a check (✔) next to the sentence that is similar in meaning to the first.

1. Ken's bicycle was hit by a car.

   _____ a. A driver was hit by Ken's bicycle.

   ✔ b. A car hit Ken's bicycle.

   _____ c. Ken hit a car with his bicycle.

2. Patients are given everything they need in the hospital.

   _____ a. Patients don't need anything in the hospital.

   _____ b. Hospitals give patients what they need.

   _____ c. Patients need a lot of things.

3. I can't lend you my jacket. It's being cleaned.

   _____ a. My jacket's dirty, so you don't want to wear it.

   _____ b. I'm going to clean my jacket, so I can't give it to you.

   _____ c. I've taken my jacket to the cleaner's, and so I can't lend it to you.

4. Am I being told the truth?

   _____ a. Are people telling me the truth?

   _____ b. Am I telling the truth?

   _____ c. Am I telling a lie?

5. Has the position* been filled?

   _____ a. Are you filling that position?

   _____ b. Have you hired* someone?

   _____ c. Have you fired* someone?

6. At a potluck meal, everyone who is invited brings something to eat or drink.

   _____ a. The people who invite others to a potluck meal buy all the food and drinks.

   _____ b. Food and drinks are brought by the people who are invited to a potluck meal.

   _____ c. The guests at a potluck meal don't prepare any food.

7. The electric bill hasn't been paid.

   _____ a. We don't need to pay the electric bill.

   _____ b. Someone has paid the electric bill.

   _____ c. No one has paid the electric bill.

8. Are you being helped?

   _____ a. Is someone helping you?

   _____ b. Did you give someone help?

   _____ c. Are you helping someone?

9. The tree was cut down after it was damaged in a storm.

   _____ a. The tree fell down during the storm.

   _____ b. People cut down the tree after the storm damaged it.

   _____ c. People cut down the tree because it caused a lot of damage.

* position: *a job*
* hire: *to give someone a job*
* fire: *to remove someone from a job, e.g., He was fired for stealing.*

Is done and *was done* (Passive)
Is being done and *has been done* (Passive)

Write answers to the questions in the passive. Use the same verb and tense used in the question.

Questions	Answers

1. Do they grow rice in Alaska?

No, rice _is grown_ in warm, wet places.

2. Who invited you to the party?

We were invited by Thomas.

3. Have they fixed your computer yet?

Yes, it _has been fixed_ already.

4. Did Einstein invent the electric light?

No, it _____
_____ by Thomas Edison.

5. How often do the companies send electric and water bills?

The bills _____
_____ every month.

6. Do they check every bag at airport security?

No, but many bags _____
_____ by security.

7. Did your son break your window?

No, it _____
_____ by another boy.

8. Is the town building a new hospital?

Yes, it _____
_____ close to here.

9. Are you using this computer?

No, but I think that _____
_____ by someone else.

10. Do they sell lottery tickets everywhere?

No, _____
_____ only at certain stores.

11. Did you cut down those trees yourself?

No, _____
_____ by a tree service.

12. *(at a hotel)* Has anyone cleaned your room yet?

Yes, it _____
_____ already.

13. *(in a store)* Is anyone helping you?

Yes, thanks, I _____
_____ .

14. Who is taking care of your children tonight?

_____
_____ by their grandmother.

REVIEW
Passive

Use your own ideas to write sentences in the passive with the words in parentheses. Use an appropriate form of the verb, and add any necessary words.

1. (building / build) _A large apartment building is being built across from the school._

2. (languages / speak) _____

3. (a good program / show) _____

4. (my favorite dish / make) _____

5. (computer / repair) _____

6. (invite / to a lot of parties) _____

7. (buildings / destroy / in the earthquake) _____

8. (music / play) _____

9. (some children / name) _____

10. (a new drug / develop) _____

UNIT 24

Be, have, and *do* in Present and Past Tenses

**Complete the conversations with *am/is/are, was/were, do/does, did,* or *has/have.*
Use *not* if necessary. Some sentences are active, and some are passive.**

1. *A:* _Did_ Karen call you last night?

   B: _Are_ you serious? Karen _hasn't_ called me for months and months.

2. *A:* _____ your jacket from Scotland?

   B: No, I think it _____ made in China, actually.

3. *A:* My brother likes his job, but he _____ like the hours.

   B: What hours _____ he work?

   A: Usually from 10 A.M. to 7 P.M., but he _____ come home until 9:30 last night.

4. *A:* I think I _____ lost my watch. _____ you seen it anywhere?

   B: No. _____ you leave it in the bathroom?

   A: No. I _____ already looked there.

   B: _____ you check your pockets?

   A: Of course.

5. *A:* _____ it raining when you left for work this morning?

   B: No. That's why I _____ take my umbrella with me this morning. Now it _____ raining and I really need it.

6. *A:* _____ you return my book to the library this morning?

   B: No, I _____ left the house all day. _____ you ask me to return it?

   A: I left you a note, but I guess you _____ see it.

   B: Sorry. Where _____ you leave it?

   A: On the refrigerator.

7. *A:* *(in a store)* _____ you been helped?

   B: Actually, I _____ just looking, thanks. But I have a question.

   A: Yes?

   B: _____ these pants and jackets sold together or separately?

   A: Separately.

   B: That's what I thought. Thanks.

Be, have, and do in Present and Past Tenses
Regular and Irregular Verbs

A. Complete these questions about a friend's new computer. Use _is/are_, _was/were_, _do/does_, _did_, or _has/have_.

1. _Did_ _____ you buy your computer at a store or directly from the company?

2. How long _____ you had your new computer?

3. Where _____ your computer made?

4. _____ you use it for work or for personal business?

5. _____ it have a lot of memory?

6. _____ you taken any computer courses?

7. _____ you thinking of getting a new printer, too?

8. _____ you also buy the desk that the computer is on?

9. _____ your computer used by other people in your family?

B. Now complete answers to the questions in Part A. Use the correct form (past tense or past participle) of the verb in parentheses.

1. I _bought_ _____ (buy) it at a local store.

2. I _____ (get) it a month ago.

3. It's American, but some of the parts _____ (come) from Mexico.

4. So far, I've _____ (use) it just for work.

5. I have never _____ (understand) computer memory, but it's a fast computer.

6. Yes, I _____ (take) a class last spring.

7. Yes, I have to because my old one _____ (break).

8. No, I _____ (find) an old desk in the basement.

9. Yes, it is _____ (use) by my children to do their homework.

EXERCISE 31

What are you doing tomorrow?

Pam is a salesperson for a computer company. She has to go to Denver next week. Look at her calendar. Use the words in parentheses to write sentences about her schedule. Use the simple present or the present continuous to tell about the future.

MONDAY	TUESDAY	WEDNESDAY
Flight to Denver: 7:50 A.M. Arrive at 9:15	9 A.M.: Meeting at Best Computer Services	Return flight to Atlanta: 6:35 A.M.
Get bus for downtown: 9:30	12:30: Lunch with my college friend Kate	Arrive Atlanta: 10:15 A.M.
11 A.M. – 5 P.M.: Work in office. Look at our company's new products; discuss products with other salespeople.	3 P.M.: Deliver and explain new computer design to City Hospital downtown	Bus from airport at 11 A.M. Take the rest of the day off*!
Go to hotel	6 P.M.: Dinner and *Hamlet* with my in-laws*. Play at 8.	

1. (fly / Denver / on Monday) *Pam is flying to Denver on Monday.*

2. (her flight to Denver / leave / at 7:50 A.M.) *Her flight to Denver leaves at 7:50 A.M.*

3. (discuss / her company's new products / in the afternoon) She _____ .

4. (not / stay / with relatives / in Denver) _____

5. (Tuesday / have / lunch / college friend) _____

6. (in the evening / go out / her in-laws) _____

* in-laws: *your husband's or wife's relatives, such as his or her parents*
* take a day off: *not to work that day*

EXERCISE CONTINUES ▶ ▶

7. (they / see / a play) _____

_____

8. (play / begin / 8) _____

_____

9. (her flight / on Wednesday / leave / very early) _____

_____

10. (return / to Atlanta / on Wednesday) _____

_____

11. (husband / not / meet / her at the airport) _____

_____

12. (her bus / depart / from the airport / at 11 A.M.) _____

_____

13. (not / go / the office / on Wednesday) _____

_____

Ms. Jenkins's class is always ready to help. Use the words in parentheses, and write (a) what Ms. Jenkins says about her *plans* for the class and (b) what the students say to *offer* help. Use *going to* for plans and *will* for offers.

1. *a.* (we / take a trip to the nature center)
   Ms. Jenkins: _We're going to take a trip to the nature center._
   b. (bring / my camera)
   Ben: _I'll bring my camera._

2. *a.* (study / Native Americans / in April)
   Ms. Jenkins: We are _____ .
   b. (bring / pictures of our family trip to Arizona)
   Barbara: I _____ .

3. *a.* (plant / a garden in the school yard in the spring)
   Ms. Jenkins: _____
   b. (bring / some seeds from home)
   Andrew and Lisa: We _____ .

4. *a.* (have / party / next month)
   Ms. Jenkins: _____
   b. (my mother / make cookies / us)
   Elizabeth: _____

Use your own ideas to write sentences. Look at the words in parentheses and discuss your plans or decisions in a sentence with *going to*. Then tell more about your plans or decisions in a sentence with *I think I will* or *I don't think I will*.

1. (buy a new car next year) *I'm not going to buy a new car next year. I don't think I will have enough money.* OR *I think I will wait for another year or two.*

2. (take a trip to Hawaii next winter) _____

3. (change jobs soon) _____

4. (take an aerobics class next month) _____

5. (visit relatives in the next two or three months) _____

6. (get some new clothes soon) _____

7. (spend a lot of money this coming year) _____

8. (move to another city in a few months) _____

Might

Rewrite the sentences. Use *might* instead of *maybe* or *perhaps*.

1. Perhaps Jason is sick again.

   Jason might be sick again.

2. Maybe we won't see you tomorrow.

   We might not see you tomorrow.

3. Maybe Nicole will be in town next week.

   Nicole might _____ .

4. Perhaps it will rain tomorrow.

   It _____ .

5. Maybe the driver doesn't know the way to our house.

   _____

6. Maybe Manuel will forget to call us.

   _____

7. Perhaps we'll go to Central America for vacation.

   _____

8. Maybe my friends will do volunteer work* this weekend.

   _____

9. Maybe you have a cold.

   _____

10. Perhaps James won't be on time for work tomorrow.

    _____

11. Maybe I'll watch TV tonight.

    _____

12. Perhaps we won't recognize Uncle Joe when we see him.

    _____

* volunteer work: *work that is not paid and that usually is done to help other people in the community*

Can and *could*

Complete the sentences with *can('t)* or *could(n't)* and one of the verbs in the box.

~~come~~	decide	find	get	play	read
sleep	speak	~~swim~~	use	~~write~~	

1. <u>Could</u> OR <u>Can</u> you <u>write</u> your address down for me, please?

2. I never go to the ocean with my friends because I <u>can't swim</u> .

3. I heard your party was a lot of fun. I'm sorry we <u>couldn't come</u> .

4. _____ I _____ your cell phone to make a call?

5. I'm looking for some sugar for my coffee, but I _____ any.

6. _____ you _____ some sugar at the store? We need some.

7. Hannah wanted to buy a new dress last night, but she _____ which one she liked better.

8. I think I'll enjoy my trip to Japan because I _____ a little Japanese.

9. Melissa's very smart. When she was four, she _____ already _____ some words in her children's books.

10. Brandon is very good at sports. He _____ soccer, football, baseball, and tennis well.

11. My apartment building was very noisy last night. I _____ .

Must

Complete the sentences with *must* or *must not* and one of the phrases in the box.

be tired	be upset	be vegetarians*	drink coffee	feel well today
have children	have enough money	know him	know it very well	like rice

1. Juan never goes out to eat with us. He _must not have enough money_ .

2. You worked 12 hours today? You _must be tired_ .

3. Sylvia never eats rice, even when we go to a Chinese restaurant. She _____
   _____ .

4. The Rileys have only lived in Miami a few weeks. They _____ .

5. Pete always orders juice or a soda when we go out. He _____ .

6. Jenny and Michael never order meat when we eat out. They _____ .

7. That actor is very famous. You _____ .

8. I saw small bikes and toys outside our new neighbors' house. They _____
   _____ .

9. Ryan's car broke down* again. He _____ .

10. Ellen's usually so friendly, but she's not today. She _____ .

   * vegetarian: *a person who does not eat meat*
   * break down: *to stop working*

Should

Look at the pictures. Write a sentence for each picture with *I think . . . should* or *I don't think . . . should* and the correct phrase from the box.

1.

2.

3.

4.

5.   6.   7.   8.

drive more carefully	ask for help to fix her flat tire	go for a walk right now
go to work today	make noise near a hospital	watch TV for such a long time
~~swim here~~	use her phone while she is driving	

1. I don't think he _should swim here_ .

2. I don't think they _____ .

3. _____

4. _____

5. _____

6. _____

7. _____

8. _____

A. Rewrite the sentences with a form of *have to*. Keep the same meaning.

1. It is necessary to pay in order to park in this lot.

    You *have to pay to park in this lot*   .

2. It is not necessary for passengers in the backseat to wear seat belts.

    Passengers in the backseat don't have to wear seat belts.

3. Is it necessary for me to take a driving test to get a license?

    Do I have to take a driving test to get a license?

4. Is it necessary for drivers to have insurance in this state?

    _____

5. It is not necessary for tourists to have a local driver's license in many places.

    _____

6. It is necessary for drivers to wear seat belts.

    _____

B. Rewrite the sentences with *must* or *must not*. (Note: you *are required* to do something = you *must* do it; you *are forbidden* to do something = you *must not* do it.)

1. You are required to have a credit card to rent a car.

    You *must have a credit card to rent a car*   .

2. You are forbidden to take pictures in the museum.

    You *must not take pictures in the museum*   .

3. Swimmers are required to take a shower before going into the pool.

    Swimmers _____ .

4. It is forbidden to park your car in front of the fire station.

    You _____ .

5. Smoking is forbidden in this building.

    You _____ .

UNIT
35

Would you like . . . ? I'd like . . .

Complete the conversations. Use *like* or *would like*. Use the words in parentheses and any other necessary words.

1. *A:* (what / you / like / for dinner) <u>*What would you like for dinner?*</u> Pasta?
   B: (not / like / pasta very much) No, I <u>*don't like pasta very much*</u> .
   A: How about fish?
   B: (like / fish a lot) Yes, I <u>*like fish a lot*</u> .

2. *A:* (you / like / your Spanish class?) _____
   B: Yes, my teacher is great.

3. *A:* (like / buy / Gary a present) I _____ .
      It's his birthday.
   B: What are going to buy for him?
   A: A CD or maybe a DVD. (like / music a lot) He _____ .

4. *A:* (what / you / like / drink?) _____
   B: Iced tea if you have any.
   A: All right. (you / like / sugar in it?) _____
   B: No, thanks.

5. *A:* (you / like / foreign movies?) _____
   B: Yes, usually. Is there one playing?
   A: Yes, a Spanish film. (you / like / go / tonight?) _____

      _____
   B: Sure. What time?

Would you like . . . ? I'd like . . .
I'd rather . . .

Complete the conversations with the words in parentheses and any other necessary ones.

1. *A:* Would you rather go shopping or stay home tonight?

   B: I have another idea. (like / go / the movies) I *'d like to go to the movies*   .

   A: (rather / stay / home) I *'d rather stay home*   . Let's rent a video.

2. *A:* (where / you / like / sit?) _____

   B: Near the front if it's OK with you.

3. *A:* Shall I tell Ana about the accident, or would you like to tell her?

   B: (rather / not / tell / her) I _____ . You do it.

4. *A:* (what / you / like / have / for dessert?) _____

   B: I think I'll just have some coffee, please.

5. *A:* Would your sister like to be a doctor?

   B: (rather / be / a teacher) Actually, she _____ .

6. *A:* Are your brother and his wife excited about moving to New York?

   B: (rather / not / move there) No, actually they _____ .
   They like Seattle.

7. *A:* Have you heard about Justin's problem?

   B: Yes. (not / like / be / in his position) I _____ .

8. *A:* Is your daughter going to go to a large college?

   B: No. (rather / go / to a small college / a large one) She _____
   _____ .

9. *A:* Shall we eat at home tonight?

   B: No. (rather / go out / eat at home) I _____ .

Do this! Don't do that! Let's do this!

Write sentences with the words in parentheses to respond to the suggestions. Make the first sentence positive and the second sentence negative. Use the base form or *Let's (not)* in the responses.

1. *A:* What shall we have for dessert?

    B: (ice cream) <u>Let's have ice cream.</u>

    (chocolate cake again) <u>Let's not have chocolate cake again.</u>

2. *A:* What should I make for dinner?

    B: (fish) <u>Make fish.</u>

    (chicken again) <u>Don't make chicken again.</u>

3. *A:* When should I pay the bills?

    B: (next week) _____

    (this week) _____

4. *A:* What should I wear to the party?

    B: (a suit and tie) _____

    (your old tennis shoes) _____

5. *A:* Whose relatives should we invite?

    B: (my relatives) _____

    (your relatives) _____

6. *A:* What should I get at the store?

    B: (some fruit and yogurt) _____

    (any cookies this time) _____

7. *A:* Where shall we go for dinner?

    B: (a new restaurant) _____

    (the same old place) _____

8. *A:* Where do you want to go for vacation?

    B: (Montreal this time) _____

    (Alaska again) _____

You are asking Michelle about her plans. Look at the questions and answers.
Then complete the list of Michelle's plans. Use *can('t)* or *might (not)* where
possible.

Your questions	Michelle's answers
1. Do you want to play tennis with us tomorrow?	Sorry, I don't have time.
2. Are you going out tonight?	Yes, I am.
3. Are you working this weekend?	I'm not sure.
4. Can you help us move on Saturday?	Yes, you can count on* me.
5. Are you going to watch the game on TV Sunday?	Yes! Definitely!*
6. Are you planting a garden next spring?	Maybe.
7. Will you be at home tomorrow night?	No, I won't.
8. Would you like to play chess this afternoon?	I'm working this afternoon.
9. Are you going to Colombia next summer?	It depends on money.
10. Are you going shopping with us on Thursday?	Sorry, I'm busy on Thursday.

List of Michelle's Plans

1. *Michelle can't play tennis with us tomorrow.*
2. *She is going out tonight.*
3. *She might work this weekend.*
4. She _____ .
5. _____
6. _____
7. _____
8. _____
9. _____
10. _____

* count on (someone): *to depend on someone*
* definitely: *for sure*

Look at the picture of a movie theater. Complete the sentences with *might*, *can/could*, *must*, *should*, *have to*, or *would like/rather* and the words in parentheses. In some cases, more than one verb is correct.

A MOVIE THEATER

1. The teenagers _should put_ (put) their feet on the floor.

2. The teenagers _shouldn't have_ (not / have) their feet on the seats.

3. The little boy _____ (like) popcorn a lot.

4. The little girl's soda _____ (fall).

5. The little girl _____ (eat) some of the little boy's popcorn.

6. This movie theater has a rule: People _____ (turn off) their cell phones. They _____ (not / use) cell phones anywhere in the theater.

7. The man _____ (not / talk) on his cell phone during the movie.

8. One woman is covering her face because she doesn't want to look at the movie. The movie _____ (be) scary.

EXERCISE CONTINUES ▶ ▶

9. A man is sleeping. He _____ (be) tired. He
_____ (not / stay awake).

10. A man is sitting behind a man with a cowboy hat. He _____
(not / see) the movie very well. He _____ (move) to another
seat.

11. A man and his wife haven't sat down yet. They _____ (not /
agree) about where to sit. Some people like to sit in the front of the theater, but other
people _____ (sit) near the back.

12. The man with the cap is looking for someone. He _____ (have)
a friend in the audience.

13. There aren't many people in the theater. The movie _____
(not / be) very popular.

Use your own ideas to complete the sentences.

1. Some people can't _drive_ OR _speak a foreign language_ OR _cook very well_ .
   Some people can't _____ .

2. As a child, I could(n't) _____ .

3. On weekends, I sometimes have to _____ .

4. I don't have to _____ this weekend, however.

5. I think parents should _____ .

6. But I don't think parents should _____ .

7. Not many people would like _____ .

8. I would rather _____ than _____ .

9. Some drivers have a lot of accidents. They must _____ .

10. In five years, the world might _____ .

11. I would not like _____ . I would rather _____
    _____ .

12. People who can't _____ should not _____
    _____ .

13. Some people make a lot of mistakes. They must not _____
    _____ .

14. If someone _____ , we might not _____ .

15. Some people would rather not _____ unless it is necessary.

There is / are

There and It

Look at the picture of the house. The information in the sentences doesn't match the picture. Rewrite each sentence to correct it.

1. There's a car in the driveway.

   There are two cars in the driveway.

2. There is a dog in the yard.

   There isn't a dog in the yard.

3. There are no mailboxes on this street.

   _____

4. There's a cat in the window.

   _____

5. There are two flower gardens in the front yard.

   _____

EXERCISE CONTINUES ▶ ▶

6. There isn't any grass in the yard.

_____

7. There are some trees in the yard.

_____

8. There's a truck in front of the house.

_____

9. There isn't a garage behind the house.

_____

10. There are no police in the neighborhood now.

_____

11. There's a bird on the chimney.

_____

12. There's a chair in the yard.

_____

13. There are two bikes against the house.

_____

14. There is a child in the yard.

_____

UNITS
38-39

There is/are
There was/were there will be there has been / have been

Complete the sentence in column B so that it has the same meaning as the sentence in column A. Use *there* in your sentences.

A	**B**
1. It isn't cloudy today.	*There aren't* _____ clouds in the sky today.
2. Did someone rob the bank?	*Was there* _____ a robbery at the bank?
3. This dessert is very sweet.	_____ a lot of sugar in the dessert.
4. My old high school has changed a lot.	_____ a lot of changes in my old high school.
5. It will be very windy this afternoon.	_____ strong winds this afternoon.
6. I couldn't sleep because it was too noisy.	I couldn't sleep because _____ too much noise.
7. A lot of people came to the meeting.	_____ a lot of people at the meeting.
8. Ice cream is a very fattening food*.	_____ a lot of fat and sugar in ice cream.
9. It has rained heavily all day.	_____ heavy rain all day.
10. I don't have any reason to go to the store. I have all the things I need right now.	_____ no reason for me to go to the store.
11. We will have to wait for the plane to arrive.	_____ a delay in the arrival of the plane.
12. The people in the next room are having a party.	_____ a party in the next room.
13. This computer had some problems.	_____ some problems with this computer.

  * fattening food: *a food that makes people fat when they eat a lot of it*

There is/are
There was/were there will be there has been / have been
It . . .

**Write B's answers to A's questions and statements. Use the words in parentheses.
Use *it* or *there* + the verb *be* in an appropriate form.**

1. *A:* How's the weather today?

    B: (a lot of wind) *There's a lot of wind.*

2. *A:* Why did it take so long to do the shopping?

    B: (a lot of people at the store) *There were a lot of people at the store.*

3. *A:* How was your flight?

    B: (long but good) *It was long but good.*

4. *A:* How's the weather today?

    B: (windy) _____

5. *A:* Is Los Angeles far from here?

    B: (almost 500 miles) _____ from here.

6. *A:* Did you enjoy your walk last night?

    B: (dark and cold) No, _____ .

7. *A:* Have you been to Denver?

    B: (a big conference there last year) Yes, _____ .

8. *A:* Did you have a good trip?

    B: (a lot of traffic on the highway) Yes, but _____ .

9. *A:* Why aren't you drinking your coffee? Isn't it good?

    B: (not hot enough) Yes, but _____ .

10. *A:* Did you take the train home last night?

    B: (a train at 9:30) Yes, _____ .

11. *A:* I'm sorry you got to the game late.

    B: I am, too. (difficult to find a parking space)_____

12. *A:* Was the movie crowded?

    B: (not many people in the ticket line) No, _____ .

UNIT
41

I am, I don't, etc.

Auxiliary Verbs

A. Answer these questions about yourself. Use *Yes, I do; No, I'm not,* etc.

1. Can you speak Chinese? _No, I can't. OR Yes, I can._
2. Have you ever been to Egypt? _Yes, I have. OR No, I haven't._
3. Do you have many relatives? _____
4. Will you be at home Saturday night? _____
5. Were you at home this morning? _____
6. Did you go out last night? _____
7. Are you working tomorrow? _____
8. Was the weather in your town nice yesterday? _____
9. Are there many parks in your town? _____
10. Have you ever eaten Thai food? _____

B. Complete the sentences with an auxiliary verb, positive or negative.

1. I feel fine today, but I _didn't_ yesterday.

2. I don't have a car, but my brother _does_ .

3. *A:* Have you eaten lunch yet?
   B: I have, but my friend _____ .

4. My best friend likes hot weather, but I _____ .

5. It didn't rain yesterday, but it _____ the day before.

6. I like living in Florida, but my family _____ .

7. My wife is from a small town, but I _____ .

8. *A:* Are you going to do your homework this afternoon?
   B: I should, but I probably _____ .

9. I've never been to India, but my parents _____ .

10. *A:* Is it going to rain today?
    B: It _____ . I don't know.

You have? / have you? you are? / are you?, etc.
Too/either and *so am I / neither do I*, etc.

Read the statement in the first column. Write a short question to show interest, in the second column. Then indicate that the same is true for you by writing *So do I*, *Neither did I*, etc. in the third column.

A friend's statement	Your short question	So / Neither . . .
1. I feel a little tired today.	*You do?*	*So do I.*
2. My sister just got married.	*She did?*	*So did I.*
3. I have never been to New York City.	*You haven't?*	*Neither have I.*
4. I stayed home last night.		
5. I'm not going to work tomorrow.		
6. I can't understand Brandon.		
7. I'll be late for work tomorrow.		
8. I'm not from Sydney.		
9. I don't like coffee very much.		
10. I've been tired lately.		
11. I'd like to take a break now.		
12. Nick couldn't go to Laurie's party.		
13. My parents don't watch much TV.		
14. My brother is very good at computers.		

You have? / have you?   you are? / are you?, etc.

Complete the sentences with a tag question. Then choose an answer from the list below.

Questions		Answers
1. Those aren't grapes, *are they*	?	*d*
2. Vicky was at work yesterday, *wasn't she*	?	*f*
3. You don't eat meat, _____	?	_____
4. You'll come to our party, _____	?	_____
5. There aren't any messages for me, _____	?	_____
6. You haven't forgotten my birthday, _____	?	_____
7. Lisa called you, _____	?	_____
8. You're not too tired to go to the movies, _____	?	_____
9. You don't like ice cream, _____	?	_____
10. You're going to work tomorrow, _____	?	_____
11. You were sick yesterday, _____	?	_____
12. Your parents aren't Mexican, _____	?	_____

Answers

  a. Yes, she did. Why?

  b. No, I'm a vegetarian*.

  c. No, I want to go.

✓d. No, they're cherries.

  e. No, they're Chilean.

✓f. Yes, I'm sure I saw her.

  g. Yes, I don't like to miss work.

  h. Yes, but I'm better now.

  i. Not especially. Do you have something else?

  j. Yes. Can I bring something?

  k. Of course not. I have a present for you.

  l. No. No one called today.

  * vegetarian: *a person who does not eat meat*

UNIT
44

Isn't . . . , haven't . . . , don't . . . , etc. (Negatives)

Rewrite the sentences so that they make sense*. Change verbs to the negative where necessary.

1. Paulo likes his boss because she isn't very nice to him.
   Paulo doesn't like his boss because she isn't very nice to him.

2. The world needs another war; it needs more peace.
   The world doesn't need another war; it needs more peace.

3. I go to bed early when I'm not sleepy.
   _____

4. Fish have wings, but birds do.
   _____

5. Read that book if you don't find it interesting.
   _____

6. You should work extra hours if you don't feel well.
   _____

7. I walked to school because the buses were running because of bad weather.
   _____

8. We ate the fish because it didn't smell very good to us.
   _____

9. They study very hard, so they don't get very good grades.
   _____

10. Sheila was here yesterday, so she didn't hear the news.
    _____

11. I'll see you tomorrow if you can't be here.
    _____

    * make sense: *to be understandable, to be logical*

Too / either and *so am I / neither do I*, etc.
Isn't . . . , haven't . . . , don't . . . , etc. (Negatives)

Complete the sentences with the words in parentheses. Use an appropriate form of the verb.

1. (I / study / last night) _I didn't study last night_____ , and neither did my friend.

2. (my son / have / a headache) _My son has a headache_____ , and so do I.

3. (my boss / be / to Canada) _____ , and neither have I.

4. (my brother / fix a car) _____ , and I can too.

5. (the Mendozas / from Mexico) _____ , and neither are the Carrillos.

6. (my car / be / for sale) _____ , and neither is my neighbor's.

7. (I / catch / the flu last year) _____ , and so did everyone else in my office.

8. (I / watch the news last night) _____ , and my wife didn't either.

9. (my father / like / his job) _____ , and neither does my brother.

10. (Tony / do / his homework now) _____ , and Julia isn't either.

11. (Edgar / be / born / in Canada) _____ , and so were his parents.

12. (I / be / at work tomorrow) _____ , and the boss won't either.

13. (I / work / a little harder) _____ , and so should you.

14. (I / like / to live in a big city) _____ , and my family wouldn't either.

EXERCISE 53

UNITS
41-44

REVIEW
Auxiliary Verbs

Complete the sentences about yourself and people you know.

1. _My friends don't get up early_ _____ , but I do.

   My neighbor doesn't have a car _____ , but I do.

   My sister doesn't teach children _____ , but I do.

   _____ , but I do.

2. A friend of mine used to work in a bank, _and I did too_ OR _and so did I_ OR _but_
   I didn't _____ .

   A friend of mine used to work in a bank, _____ .

3. _____ , and so does my friend.

4. _____ , and so am I.

5. _____ , but I did.

6. Some people don't like dogs, _____ .

7. _____ , but I haven't.

8. _____ , but someone might.

9. Many people have musical talent, _____ .

10. _____ , and so will I.

11. _____ , and neither has my friend.

12. _____ , but a few have.

13. _____ , but she said she was going to.

14. Most people that I know don't like to work, _____ .

15. _____ , but I wouldn't.

16. Some people are not good writers, _____ .

17. _____ , and so did I.

UNIT
45

Is it . . . ?, Have you . . . ?, Do they . . . ?, etc.

Questions

Your friend is taking a trip. Complete the questions.

Your friend says:	You ask:
1. We're going to Hawaii.	When _are you going_ ?
2. We would like to visit more than one island there.	Which islands _____ ?
3. I've bought some things for the trip.	What things _____ ?
4. Our plane leaves very early.	What time _____ ?
5. It takes a long time to fly to Hawaii.	How long _____ ?
6. The tickets didn't cost very much.	How much _____ ?
7. I haven't told my parents about the trip.	Why _____ ?
8. We take a few trips every year.	How many _____ ?
9. We went to Puerto Rico recently.	When _____ ?
10. We also traveled someplace else a few months ago.	Where _____ ?
11. We were planning to go to Mexico.	Where in Mexico _____ ?
12. We changed our minds about going there.	Why _____ ?
13. We've been there before.	How many times _____ ?
14. We go there often.	How often _____ ?
15. I have a lot of vacation time.	How much _____ ?

UNIT 46

Who saw you? Who did you see?

Write questions. Ask about the underlined word.

Statements	Questions
1. <u>SOMEONE</u> is getting married next week.	Who *is getting married next week* ?
2. I called <u>SOMEONE</u> last night.	Who *did you call last night* ?
3. I saw <u>SOMETHING</u>.	What _____ ?
4. <u>SOMETHING</u> is happening.	What _____ ?
5. <u>SOMETHING</u> happened to me yesterday.	What _____ ?
6. <u>SOMEONE</u> lives in a castle.	Who _____ ?
7. My neighbors have <u>SOMETHING</u>.	What _____ ?
8. <u>SOMETHING</u> woke me up this morning.	What _____ ?
9. I eat <u>SOMETHING</u> for breakfast every morning.	What _____ ?
10. I know <u>SOMEONE</u>.	Who _____ ?
11. <u>SOMEONE</u> teaches physics.	Who _____ ?
12. I asked <u>SOMEONE</u> for directions.	Who _____ ?
13. <u>SOMEONE</u> fixed the broken window.	Who _____ ?
14. We need <u>SOMETHING</u> for the recipe.	What _____ ?
15. <u>SOMETHING</u> surprised us yesterday.	What _____ ?

Who is she talking to? What is it like?

A. Complete the conversations with the verb in parentheses and a preposition. Use any other necessary words.

1. *A:* Mary Jo is talking on the phone again!

   B: Who *is she talking to* _____ (talk)?

   A: I don't know.

2. *A:* What are you doing?

   B: Waiting.

   A: What _____ (wait)?

   B: For the mail.

3. *A:* Are these your books?

   B: No, they're not.

   A: Who _____ (belong)?

   B: To that man over there, I think.

4. *A:* Are you busy?

   B: Yes, I'm writing a letter.

   A: Who _____ (write)?

   B: To a friend from school.

5. *A:* Can I borrow your dictionary?

   B: Sorry, I don't have it. I lent it to someone.

   A: Who _____ (lend)?

   B: To my brother.

6. *A:* How was your trip?

   B: Great. We loved our hotel.

   A: Which _____ (stay)?

   B: At the Biltmore.

7. *A:* I saw a great old movie last night.

   B: What _____ (be)?

   A: It was about a bank robbery.

EXERCISE CONTINUES ▶ ▶

8. *A:* I don't understand how you can travel alone.

   B: I'm not traveling alone.

   A: Oh? Who _____ (travel)?

   B: With my cousin.

B. Now write questions with *What is/are . . . like*? or *What was/were . . . like*?

1. *A:* We have some new neighbors.

   B: *What are they like?* _____ (they)

   A: They seem friendly.

2. *A:* We went to the beach in Florida.

   B: *What was the water like?* _____ (the water)

   A: Warm and wonderful.

3. *A:* We drove on the freeways of Los Angeles last week.

   B: Really? _____ (the traffic)

   A: It was scary*. The cars move really fast.

4. *A:* I finally met my wife's family.

   B: _____ (they)

   A: They're nice people.

5. *A:* I really liked my students last semester.

   B: Good. _____ (they)

   A: They loved to learn, and they loved to laugh.

   * scary: *frightening, making you afraid, e.g., a scary movie*

What . . . ?, Which . . . ?, and How . . . ?
How long does it take . . . ?

Complete the questions. Read the answers first.

Questions	Answers
1. _What color_ is your car?	It's red.
2. _Which_ car is yours?	The blue one.
3. _____ does the library open?	It opens at 10 A.M.
4. _____ is the Empire State Building?	It's 1,250 feet tall.
5. _____ is your car?	There's room for four people.
6. _____ of fruit would you like?	I'd like an apple, please.
7. _____ is it to your office?	It's exactly 12 miles from here.
8. _____ is bigger, Los Angeles or Mexico City?	Mexico City.
9. _____ of job does Sally have?	She's an accountant.
10. _____ does it rain here?	It rains almost every day in the winter.
11. _____ was your TV?	It was around $300.
12. _____ would you like, tea or coffee? I have both.	I'd like coffee, please.
13. _____ is your brother?	He's six feet four inches tall.
14. _____ is older, Paula or her husband?	Paula.
15. _____ does it take to drive to San Francisco?	About nine hours.

What . . . ?, Which . . . ?, and How . . . ?
How long does it take . . . ?

Write questions with *What*, *Which*, *How*, etc. They should have the same meaning as the questions on the left.

1. Is your sister 12? 15? *How old is your sister?*

2. Did you get up early? Late? *What time did you get up?*

3. Is this sweater a large or a medium? What _____ ?

4. Did you spend $20 on the present? $30? _____

5. Do you like this shirt? Or that one? _____

6. Have you been working here a long time? A short time? _____

7. Do you like popular music? Classical? Jazz? _____

8. Do you go to church every week? Once a month? _____

9. Are her eyes brown? Green? Blue? _____

10. Is the brown coat yours? The blue one? _____

11. Does it take a year to learn a language? Two years? _____

12. Were the flowers $10? $15? _____

13. Will it take you an hour to drive to the beach? Two hours? _____

14. Should we buy roses? Violets? _____

15. Did it take you a week to paint your house? Two weeks? _____

EXERCISE 59

Do you know where . . . ?, I don't know what . . . , etc.

Write answers to the questions. Begin with any one of the following:
• *I think I know . . .* • *I'm not sure . . .* • *I don't know . . .* • *No one knows . . .*

1. Where is Ashgabad?   *I think I know where Ashgabad is.*

2. Do fish have teeth?   *I don't know if fish have teeth.*
   OR *I don't know whether fish have teeth.*

3. How many stars are there in the sky?   *No one knows how many stars there are in the sky.*

4. What does "silly" mean?

5. Who was Abraham Lincoln?

6. How does a computer work?

7. Who did John F. Kennedy marry?

8. How many times have astronauts gone to the moon?

9. When was Mother Teresa born?

10. How long does it take to fly from Beijing to New York City?

11. How much does a house in Moscow cost?

12. How many calories are there in an apple?

13. Why do people make war?

14. How many people have died in wars?

15. Did it rain more a hundred years ago?

Write questions about a family. It can be about a real family or a family from a book. It can be a famous family or your own family.

1. Where *do the Westons usually go on vacation in summer* ?

   Where _____ ?

2. What *did the Weston family do last summer* ?

   What _____ ?

3. When _____ ?

4. Why _____ ?

5. Is _____ ?

6. Do _____ ?

7. Can someone tell me which _____ ?

8. Does anyone know what kind of _____ ?

9. Did _____ ?

10. Have _____ ?

11. _____ , does he?

12. _____ , didn't they?

13. How long does it take _____ ?

UNIT
51

She said that . . . He told me that . . .

Look at the pictures. They show what the people really did. Read what the people said. Complete the sentences about what they said and what they did. Use *said* or *told*.

1. Frank and Ashley said, "We'll be home early."

   Frank and Ashley <u>said that they would be home early</u>, but they got home very late.

2. Kate said, "I am a vegetarian*."

   Kate <u>told</u> me that _____, but the last time we were in a restaurant together she ordered chicken.

3. Larry said, "I am very sick today."

   _____ that _____

   _____, but someone saw him at a baseball game.

4. Matt said, "I have to visit my aunt in the hospital."

   _____ me that

   _____,

   but he went out dancing last night.

5. Alex and Susan said, "We are going to get up early on Saturday."

   _____ that _____

   _____, but they slept late.

   * vegetarian: *a person who doesn't eat meat*

EXERCISE CONTINUES ▶▶

6. Mrs. Holden said, "My son can play the violin beautifully."

_____ us that _____

_____ ,

but I don't think he can.

7. Bill's aunt said, "I have just sent you some money for your birthday."

Last week _____ that

_____ , but he hasn't

received it.

8. Richard said, "I won't tell anyone your secret."

Richard _____ me

that _____ ,

but he told everyone.

9. Aunt Claudia said, "I don't eat sweets."

_____ that

_____ ,

but most of the chocolates are gone.

Work/working, go/going, do/doing

Complete the sentences so that they correctly describe the situation.

1. It rained this morning, so Leslie stayed home.

    Leslie stayed home because it was _*raining*_____ this morning.

2. My parents are thinking of leaving town this weekend.

    My parents might _*leave town this weekend*_____ .

3. My advice to you is, "Study harder."

    I think you should _____ .

4. I had trouble sleeping last night.

    I didn't _____ well _____ .

5. "I would love to go with you, but I have to watch my little brother now," Bob said.

    Bob can't _____ us because he is _____ right now.

6. *(on the phone)* Sorry, Adam isn't in right now. He's gone to lunch.

    Adam is _____ lunch outside the office.

7. It's late. I don't think your parents are awake anymore.

    It's late. Your parents must _____ asleep already.

8. Yesterday Jean said, "I need to do some shopping, but I don't have any money."

    Jean wanted _____ , but she didn't _____ .

9. Judy called to talk to Gloria, but Gloria was in the bathtub.

    Judy couldn't _____ because Gloria was _____ a bath.

10. *Sid:* Does Ben still work for his brother?

    Nat: No, he got another job a few months ago.

    Ben used _____ , but he doesn't anymore.

11. *Lucy:* Do you want to go to lunch now?

    Clare: No, I need to wait for an important phone call.

    Clare isn't going to lunch now because she has _____ for a phone call.

To . . . (I want to do) and –ing (I enjoy doing)

Complete the sentences so that they correctly describe the situation. Use *to . . .* or *-ing*.

1. I asked Jeremy for help. He said, "No."

    _Jeremy_____ refused _to help me_____ .

2. Do you like to stay home on weekends?

    _Do you_____ enjoy _staying home on weekends_____ ?

3. My brother dreams of visiting Egypt one day.

    My brother would love _____ .

4. Could you give me a ride* to the doctor's tomorrow afternoon?

    Would you mind _____ ?

5. *Marlene:* Would you like me to give you a ride* home?

    You: No, thanks. I'd rather walk.

    Marlene offered _____ , but I preferred _____ .

6. *Elena:* Should we leave at seven tomorrow morning?

    Steve: How about 7:30? Seven is a little early.

    Elena suggested _____ , but Steve wanted _____ .

7. *Dan:* Let's go to the movies.

    Jean: Not right now. I want to finish writing my report for work.

    Dan wanted _____ , but Jean didn't want to

    stop _____ .

8. *Mother:* Why are you watching TV? Did you clean your room?

    Bev: Yes. I've cleaned it already.

    Bev has finished _____ .

9. How about going to the mountains this weekend?

    Would you like _____ ?

10. "A lawyer has a very boring job. I would rather be a teacher," Jim said.

    Jim would hate _____ a lawyer. He'd prefer _____ .

    * give someone a ride: *to take someone somewhere in a car*

UNITS
53-54

To . . . (I want to do) and -ing (I enjoy doing)
I want you to . . . and I told you to . . .

Read the conversation. Then complete the description of the conversation. Use to . . . or -ing.

1. *Sylvia:* Use your credit card to pay for the tickets. It's faster.

   Nathan: You're right, but I think I'll pay by check.

   She told *him to use his credit card to pay for the tickets* . He decided *to pay by check* .

2. *Mother:* Can't you pick up your dirty clothes?

   Son: I guess I can, but I don't want to.

   The mother wanted _____ , but he refused _____ them up.

3. *Martin:* Let's go to the beach on Saturday.

   Wanda: OK, I like to be out in the sun on weekends.

   He suggested _____ . She said she enjoyed _____ .

4. *Jonathan:* I don't know why you don't want to buy this jacket. It looks nice on you.

   Jennie: I think it's too expensive, but I'll buy it if you think I should.

   Jonathan persuaded _____ the jacket, which she didn't want _____ at first.

5. *Jason:* Officer, can I leave now?

   Police officer: No, you'll have to wait.

   The police officer made _____ .

6. *Boss:* Can you work on Saturday?

   Bert: That's fine. I don't have anything else to do.

   The boss asked _____ , and Bert didn't mind _____ that day.

UNIT
55

I went to the store to . . .

Complete the sentences, keeping the same meaning. Use _to_ and _for_ where necessary.

1. I'm not going to Miami for Christmas. It costs too much.

   I don't have enough money _to go to Miami for Christmas_ .

2. I'm standing here because I need to ask the teacher about the test.

   I'm waiting to _____ .

3. Nicole flew to Quebec to go to a wedding.

   Nicole flew to Quebec for _____ .

4. I went to Ellen's party because I wanted to relax and meet new people.

   I went to Ellen's party to _____ .

5. Can you help me with my Arabic? Or are you too busy?

   Do you have enough time _____ .

6. I can't leave yet. The babysitter* hasn't come yet.

   I'm waiting _____ come.

7. Ron borrowed $20 from me for a present.

   Ron borrowed $20 from me to _____ .

8. When I finish this book, I'm going to give it to Wally. He's waiting.

   Wally is waiting for _____ the book.

9. Sophie is taking a class. She is learning how to use a computer.

   Sophie is taking a class to _____ .

10. Mrs. Nickels went to Brazil. She went to a conference there.

    Mrs. Nickels went to Brazil for _____ .

11. Answer my question. I'm waiting.

    I'm waiting for _____ my question.

    * babysitter: _person who takes care of children in their home when the parents are out_

Use your own ideas to complete the sentences. Begin your answer with a verb in the base form (*work/go*), *to . . .* (*to work / to go*), or *-ing* (*working/going*).

1. When visitors come to my town, I usually suggest _visiting the museum downtown_ .

   When visitors come to my town, I usually suggest _going to the mountains near the city_ .

   When visitors come to my town, I usually suggest _staying in one of our nice, old hotels_ .

   When visitors come to my town, I usually suggest _____ .

2. A lot of people want _____ .

3. When I was little, I used _____ .

4. I can't _____ because _____ .

5. My friends and I couldn't _____ because we didn't _____ .

6. I usually enjoy _____ .

7. When I am busy, I sometimes forget _____ .

8. If you want _____ well, you need _____ .

9. I hate _____ , but I don't mind _____ .

10. The father often told his children, "I want you _____

    _____ , but I don't want you _____ ."

11. I wanted _____ , but I couldn't persuade _____ .

12. Sometimes people ask me _____ .

13. I am learning English _____ .

14. I refused _____ because _____ .

15. Sometimes I think I should _____ because I don't _____ .

16. I would like _____ , but it might _____ .

REVIEW
-ing and *to*

Use your own ideas to complete the sentences. Add a verb in the base form (*work/go*), *to* . . . (*to work / to go*), or *-ing* (*working/going*).

1. I don't mind <u>*traveling alone*</u> , but I really prefer <u>*to travel with other people*</u>
   OR <u>*traveling with other people*</u>   .
   I don't mind _____ , but I really prefer _____ .

2. I was _____ when someone started _____ .

3. I used _____ , but I don't _____ anymore.

4. I can't _____ because I am _____ .

5. I love _____ , but I don't enjoy _____ .

6. They didn't let _____ because they expected _____ .

7. My doctor often advises _____ , but I sometimes
   forget _____ .

8. I couldn't persuade _____ , so I tried _____ .

9. My teacher suggested _____ , but I couldn't _____ .

10. I didn't _____ , and I don't _____ .

11. I was planning _____ , but I decided _____ .

12. I should _____ , but I will probably _____ instead.

13. I can _____ , but I would hate _____ .

14. My boss asked _____ , but he didn't make _____ .

15. I went _____ for _____ .

UNIT 56

Go to . . . go on . . . go for . . . go -ing

Go, Get, Do, Make, and Have

Use *go* in an appropriate form and the correct word(s) from the box to complete the sentences. Use *to*, *on*, or *for* if necessary.

a business trip	a movie	drugstore / some aspirin	strike*	shopping	skiing
Poland / vacation	~~swimming~~	~~the supermarket~~	a walk	work	

1. It's hot. Why don't we _go swimming_ ?

2. *(on the phone)* I can't talk to you now. I have to _go to the supermarket_
   to buy some rice and other things for dinner.

3. The Thompsons _____ last week. They are
   visiting relatives there.

4. We _____ in Colorado next winter if there's enough snow.

5. We need some exercise. Let's _____ before dinner.

6. Mrs. Lopez travels a lot in her job. In fact, she's _____
   to New York later this week.

7. *A:* Where's Ariana?

   B: She has _____ for some birthday presents.
   She'll be back soon.

8. What time are you _____ tomorrow? I need a
   ride to the library next to your office.

9. I'd like to go out with you tonight, but I'm _____
   with a friend. You can join us if you want.

10. I'm _____ . Do we need anything else?

11. That shoe factory isn't producing anything. The workers _____
    last week.

    * strike: *refusal to work*

Complete the sentences with the correct form of *get* and the words in parentheses. Sometimes you need to add *in, on, off, out of,* or *to*.

1. *A:* Are you ready to leave yet?

   B: No, I still have to _get dressed_ (dressed).

2. *A:* Is that young couple married?

   B: Yes. They _____ (married) last year.

3. I'm _____ (tired). I think I'll go to bed.

4. I couldn't find a seat when I _____ (the bus) this morning.

   But I found a seat when some people _____ (the bus) at the museum.

5. Poor Diane. She forgot her briefcase when she _____ (the taxi) this morning.

6. Can I stand under your umbrella? I'm _____ (wet).

7. *A:* *(in an office)* Hello, I'm here to see Mrs. Rossi.

   B: One minute, please. I'll _____ (her) for you.

8. *A:* What time shall I call you?

   B: I usually _____ (home) about 5:30, so any time after that.

9. *A:* Sorry I didn't _____ (here) earlier to help out. I took the wrong turn and _____ (lost).

   B: That's all right. We are still _____ (ready) for the party. You can help us with some last-minute things.

10. *A:* We're going skiing in the mountains this weekend.

    B: How nice. How long does it take to _____ (there)?

    A: About three hours.

11. My boss will be angry if I _____ (work) late again.

12. Five people _____ (the car) before Reggie, so there was no room for him.

Complete the paragraphs with the correct form of *do* or *make*.

Last week I 1) _made_ a stupid mistake. While I was 2) _____ the dishes one morning, my tooth started to hurt. It was too early to call the dentist, so I asked my brother, "Can you 3) _____ me a favor?"

"Sure, what is it?" he asked.

"Could you 4) _____ a phone call for me later? I need to 5) _____ an appointment with Dr. Greer, but I have a lot to 6) _____ at the office this morning, and I won't have time to call," I said.

"I'll 7) _____ my best to get you an appointment. What day do you want it for?" he asked.

"Tomorrow is OK, but if he can see me this afternoon, so much the better," I answered. I 8) _____ a little more housework and then left for work. But my toothache was getting worse.

I called my brother from work at lunchtime. "What are you 9) _____ ?" I asked.

"I just finished 10) _____ my laundry, and now I'm 11) _____ myself lunch. I called Dr. Greer, and he can see you at 4 P.M. today," my brother said.

"I'm lucky he can see me today," I said. "Thanks for 12) _____ this for me. I'll see you after my appointment."

When I got to my dentist's office, I realized what I had 13) _____ . My dentist's name is Dr. Philips. I had asked my brother to call Dr. Greer, my regular doctor, not my dentist. I still had a toothache, and Dr. Philips's office was closed for the day. "What should I 14) _____ now?" I thought to myself. In the end, I just went home, took two aspirins, asked my brother not to 15) _____ too much noise, and went to bed.

Luckily, my toothache was gone the next morning. I didn't have to see the dentist this time, but I know that I'll have to 16) _____ something about my tooth soon.

UNIT
59

Have

What do you say in these situations? Use *have* or *have got* in the correct form and the words in parentheses.

1. Your friend had a party for her mother's birthday. Ask your friend where it was.

   (you / the party) _Where did you have the party?_

2. Your sister is holding her head and looks sick. What do you ask her?

   (a headache) _Do you have a headache?_ OR _Have you got a headache?_

3. Andrew lost his driver's license. He had a lot of accidents. Ask him about the accidents.

   (How many) _____

4. You arrive home late with your brother. You can't find your key. Ask your brother about his key.

   (your key) _____

5. Eric looks a little nervous when he gets off the plane. Ask about his flight.

   (bad) _____

6. Your friend's sister was expecting a baby the last time you saw her. Ask about the baby.

   (your sister / her baby / yet) _____

7. Your friend Sarah hasn't talked to her brother for six months. Perhaps there was an argument.* Ask her.

   (you / with) _____

8. Mike missed work last week. Many other people were out with the flu. Ask Mike if that was his problem.

   (last week) _____

9. Your friends just came home from a concert. What do you ask them?

   (a good time / at the concert) _____

   * argument: *a fight, a disagreement*

REVIEW
Go, get, do, make, and *have*

Complete the conversations with the correct form of *do, get, have,* or *make*.

1. *A:* Who _does_ _____ the cooking at your house?

   B: My dad. My mom _gets_ _____ home from work too late to cook.

2. *A:* Does your husband _____ housework?

   B: Not often. He _____ dinner on the weekends, but I

   have to _____ all the cleaning.

   A: But you _____ a job now. That doesn't seem fair.

   B: It isn't. But his mother _____ everything for him when he was young. He has

   been that way since we _____ married.

3. *A:* Who's _____ all that noise?

   B: The students next door must be _____ a party again.

   Stay calm – don't _____ angry.

   A: It's hard to _____ my homework with that loud music playing. I know

   I'll _____ a lot of mistakes because I just can't concentrate* with all

   the noise.

   B: I'll _____ dressed and go next door to ask them to be quiet.

4. *A:* *(on a bus)* Let's _____ off the bus at the next stop. I'm _____

   tired of standing – I'd rather walk.

   B: Look, you can _____ that seat. There's a free one over there now. I'll stand.

5. *A:* Tomorrow morning, can you remind me to _____ a phone call?

   B: Sure. Who do you need to call?

   A: The dentist. I need to _____ an appointment for a cleaning.

6. *A:* Did you _____ a good time in Florida?

   B: Yes, it was wonderful. We _____ breakfast by the ocean every

   morning. We didn't have to _____ laundry or the dishes.

   In fact, we didn't _____ any work all week. We didn't even have to

   _____ our beds.

   A: Lucky you!

* concentrate: *to keep your attention on something*

REVIEW
Go, get, do, make, and have

Use your own ideas to write sentences with the words in parentheses.

1. (do housework / never) *We never do housework on Saturday.*
   OR *I never did housework before, but I have to do it now.*

2. (go to bed / late) _____

3. (get to work / early) _____

4. (get married / soon) _____

5. (have a baby / not long ago) _____

6. (go shopping / at lunchtime) _____

7. (have an accident / a while ago) _____

8. (make / a terrible mistake) _____

9. (have a party / on my birthday) _____

10. (get ready / after) _____

11. (do exercises / at night) _____

12. (make a list / before) _____

I/me, he/him, they/them, etc.

Pronouns and Possessives

**Complete the conversations. Use an appropriate form of like *(like/likes,
don't/doesn't like,* or *do/does . . . like).* Use the correct form of pronouns *(I/me,
you, she/her, etc.).***

A's Statement or Question	**B's Response**
1. Why doesn't Laurie eat spaghetti?	*She doesn't like it.*
2. I met my fiancé's parents last night.	Really? *Do you like them?*
3. Eric is really nice, and so is his sister.	I agree. _____ both a lot.
4. Are those your new shoes?	Yes. _____ ?
5. My sons are taking swimming lessons at the park.	Really? _____ ?
6. Samantha, you never eat food from the cafeteria. Why not?	Well, _____ very much.
7. Why does Jim's dog bark every time we visit?	Maybe _____ .
8. Does your brother want to go to college in the west or in the east?	The west. _____ better.
9. Why does Liz want to sell her sofa?	_____ anymore. She wants to buy a new one.
10. I always invite Ahmed and his family when we have a party.	It seems that you _____ a lot.
11. Would your father like cream in his coffee?	Yes. _____ black.
12. Is Sarah going to buy that expensive jacket?	No. _____ , but she doesn't have enough money to buy it.
13. So, why don't you eat tomatoes?	_____ , but I can't eat them. They make me feel sick.
14. Are the Simons going to eat at their usual restaurant?	No. _____ anymore. They say the prices have gone up a lot, and the food isn't as good as it was.

EXERCISE 75

I/me, he/him, they/them, etc.

Complete the questions with *I*, *me*, *he*, *him*, etc.

1. Carol wants to borrow Bob's car. Will he lend *it*   to *her* ?

2. I'd like to meet Mrs. Chang. Would you introduce *her* to *me* ?

3. The Kennedys want to see your house. Will you show _____ to _____ ?

4. I'd like to borrow your car. Will you lend _____ to _____ ?

5. My parents want to go to a concert Saturday night. Can you take _____ to _____ ?

6. We don't understand pages 22 to 24. Will the teacher explain _____ to _____ ?

7. I didn't see the accident. Could you describe _____ to _____ ?

8. The police didn't see the woman who left the scene of the accident*. Can you describe _____ to _____ ?

9. You want to look at my newspaper? I can lend _____ to _____ for a few minutes.

10. My mother would like to see the flowers in George's garden. Do you think he will show _____ to _____ ?

11. They didn't hear the joke. Can you tell _____ to _____ ?

12. I left my papers in your office. Would you bring _____ to _____ ?

13. Dad left his lunch at home. Can you take _____ to _____ ?

14. I'd like some butter, please. Can you pass _____ to _____ ?

15. Sally would like some more beans. Could you pass _____ to _____ ?

16. I didn't get Mr. Ricci's e-mail. Can you send _____ to _____ ?

17. Richard didn't understand the directions. Can you explain _____ to _____ again?

18. Miranda doesn't know our friends. Can you introduce _____ to _____ ?

* scene of the accident: *place where the accident happened*

My/his/their, etc.
Whose is this? It's mine/yours/theirs, etc.
I, me, my, and *mine*

Read the situation. Check (✔) the best description.

1. We took their luggage to his hotel room.

   _✔_ a. My parents had a suitcase. We left it in my brother's room at the hotel.

   _____ b. My sister had a lot of luggage, so we helped her to the room with it.

   _____ c. My two brothers each had a suitcase. We needed room in the car, so we put the suitcases in my sister's room.

2. She used your towel. Why don't you use hers?

   _____ a. You can use Sarah's towel because she used yours by mistake.

   _____ b. Don't use Sarah's towel. There's another one that John hasn't used yet.

   _____ c. I'll give you and Sarah clean towels.

3. Ours is broken, so she used theirs.

   _____ a. Our lawn mower* isn't working. Anna borrowed her son's lawn mower.

   _____ b. Anna didn't have a lawn mower, so she borrowed one from us.

   _____ c. Anna borrowed our neighbors' lawn mower because our lawn mower needs to be repaired.

4. Yours is difficult, but I think hers is more difficult.

   _____ a. Your job is easier than Jane's.

   _____ b. I think you worker harder than Jane.

   _____ c. Ted and Jane have harder jobs than you do.

5. Mine are blue, but his are brown.

   _____ a. I have a blue suitcase, but my brother has a brown one.

   _____ b. Joe has brown suitcases. I have blue suitcases.

   _____ c. Sarah's suitcases are brown, but my suitcases are blue.

6. *A:* Is this his or hers?

   B: Neither. It's ours.

   _____ a. The keys don't belong to John or Maria; they belong to us.

   _____ b. This key belongs to John and Maria.

   _____ c. This key belongs to us, not to John or Maria.

   * lawn mower: *a machine used for cutting grass*

My/his/their, etc.
Whose is this? It's mine/yours/theirs, etc.
I, me, my, and mine

Read the paragraphs. Then complete them with I, me, my, mine, etc.

Barbara, a co-worker, can be a difficult person. Recently, I lent Barbara 1) _my_
pen at work because she didn't have 2) _hers_ that day. But 3) _it_
was a present from a friend, so I wanted 4) _____ back. I asked 5) _____
to return 6) _____ as soon as possible. Yesterday she told 7) _____
that she had lost the pen. She's so careless!

I am not the only person who has a problem with Barbara. Just last week Ben gave
8) _____ extra pair of reading glasses to 9) _____ because she had
left 10) _____ at home. She promised 11) _____ that she would
return 12) _____ the next day, but Ben still doesn't have his glasses.

One time, Barbara asked two co-workers for part of 13) _____ lunch.
"I forgot 14) _____ on the train," she explained. They generously gave her
some of 15) _____ . Then she borrowed a dollar from 16) _____
to get something to drink! They weren't very happy.

Yesterday was the worst! She came into 17) _____ office and took my chair.
When I asked her what she was doing, she said, "I didn't know it was 18) _____ .
I thought it was 19) _____." She's impossible.

UNIT
64

Myself/yourself/themselves, etc.

Look at the picture. Rewrite the sentences to correct them. Use pronouns ending with *–self* or *–selves* or *each other* where possible.

AT THE PARK

1. A young woman is sitting by herself.

   A young man is sitting by himself.

2. Two women are sitting on the same bench and talking to themselves.

   _____

3. The girls on the swings are enjoying themselves.

   _____

4. The young man and young woman on rollerblades are waving at themselves.

   _____

EXERCISE CONTINUES ▶ ▶

5. The child is saying, "I want to feed the pigeons by herself."

_____

6. A girl with a dog is angry at herself. The dog is enjoying itself, however.

_____

7. The boy with the skateboard hurt someone when he fell.

_____

8. The woman is telling her two friends, "Enjoy yourself at the park."

_____

–'s *(Kate's camera / my brother's car, etc.)*

Use a word or phrase from the box and the words in parentheses to complete each sentence.

the bottom	the color	the condition	doctor
~~husband~~	in-laws*	job	little girl and boy
names	party	~~roof~~	wives

1. *My aunt's husband* _____ (my aunt) is a nice man.

2. *The roof of this building* _____ (this building) needs repair.

3. _____ (my father) isn't interesting, but the salary is good.

4. We had fun at _____ (Susan), but she didn't enjoy herself much because she was busy with serving food.

5. _____ (my uncles) are lawyers.

6. _____ (your package) is wet. Is there a bottle inside?

7. Do you see _____ (brother) very often, or do he and his family live far away?

8. I didn't recognize you! You changed _____ (your hair).

9. Mikey and Annie are really _____ (children). We would usually call adults Mike and Ann.

10. _____ (my son) are coming to dinner. I've never met them before.

11. My dentist said, " _____ (your teeth) is terrible."

12. _____ (Kathy) told her she was in perfect health.

* in-laws: *your husband's or wife's relatives, such as his or her parents*

Use your own ideas to write sentences with the words in parentheses.

1. (his / my / mine) *My brother likes his English teacher, but I think mine is better.*
   OR My friend lost her calculator, so she borrowed mine.

2. (my friend's / him) _____

3. (the beginning / the story) _____

4. (my parents' / them) _____

5. (ourselves / hurt) _____

6. (themselves / him) _____

7. (by yourselves / with each other) _____

8. (each other / angry) _____

9. (hers / my) _____

10. (theirs / mine) _____

11. (think / himself) _____

12. (the telephone number / that company) _____

13. (they / us / it) _____

UNITS
66-67

A/an . . .
Flower(s) and bus(es) (Singular and Plural)

A and The

The information in the sentences doesn't match the picture. Correct the sentences. Use the appropriate form (singular or plural) of the nouns and verbs in the sentences. Use *a/an* correctly.

1. There's a mirror on the wall of the restaurant.

   There are two mirrors on the wall of the restaurant.

2. There are two families in the restaurant.

   There is a family in the restaurant.

3. This is a Chinese restaurant.

   _____

4. There's a child in the family.

   _____

5. The mother is wearing shorts.

   _____

6. The boy is wearing long pants and a shirt.

   _____

7. There is a flower on each table.

   _____

EXERCISE CONTINUES ▶ ▶

8. There's a shelf on the back wall of the restaurant.

_____

9. There's a dish on the top shelf.

_____

10. There are a knife, a fork, and a spoon on the middle shelf.

_____

11. There's a bowl with some apples on the bottom shelf.

_____

12. There are some mice under one of the tables.

_____

13. The restaurant is open for an hour at lunchtime.

_____

14. Two women are ordering food.

_____

15. There's a fish in the fish tank.

_____

UNITS
66-69

A/an . . .
Flower(s) and bus(es) (Singular and Plural)
A car, some money (Countable and Uncountable)

Complete the sentences with the words in parentheses and *a/an* or *–s* if necessary.

1. (oil, stove, tea, teapot, tomato, water)
   a. To make tea, you need *a stove, tea, a teapot, and water* .
   b. You don't need *oil or tomatoes* OR *oil or a tomato* .

2. (computer, glue, place to work, ruler, tool, university class, wood)

   ruler

   glue

   tools

   a. To make a chair, you need _____

   _____ .

   b. You don't need _____

   _____ .

3. (dentist, guitar, long hair, lesson, person to listen, orchestra, piano, piece of music, teacher, test, time to practice)
   a. To learn to play the guitar, it is helpful to have _____

   _____ .

   b. You don't need _____

   _____ .

EXERCISE CONTINUES ▶ ▶

4. (blanket, car, carpet, diamond, dish, fork, furniture, money, pillow, pot and pan, refrigerator, stove, towel, vegetable)

a. To furnish an apartment, a couple needs _____

_____ .

b. They don't need _____

_____ .

5. (engineer, garden, hammer, knife, scissors, seed, shovel, soil, water)

shovel

a. To grow flowers, you need _____

_____ .

b. You don't need _____

_____ .

6. (dictionary, idea, information, new hat, paper, time to think, TV program)

a. To write an essay, a student needs _____

_____ .

b. A student doesn't need _____

_____ .

A car, some money (Countable and Uncountable)

Complete the sentences with the nouns in parentheses and *a/an* or *–s* where necessary. Use *some* where possible.

1. (music, walk)

   A: To relax, I sometimes take *a walk* _____ .

   B: Really? I just listen to *some music* _____ when I'm nervous.

2. (piece of chicken, rice)

   A: What did you have for dinner?

   B: Just _____ and _____ .

3. (bread, can of beans)

   A: What did you buy at the store?

   B: _____ and two _____ .

4. (long brown hair, small nose, eye)

   A: How will I know your daughter when I see her?

   B: She has _____ , _____ and blue _____ .

5. (new suitcase, warm clothing)

   A: What do we need for our trip?

   B: We need _____ and two _____ .

6. (bottle of perfume, earring)

   A: What would Gloria like for her birthday?

   B: I'm not sure. I bought her _____ and _____ .

7. (ice cream, apple)

   A: (at the supermarket) Should we buy _____ ? They look good.

   B: No, I'd rather get _____ .

8. (glass of water, lemonade)

   A: I've drunk three _____ and I'm still thirsty.

   B: Why don't you have _____ ?

A/an and the
Go to work   go home   go to the movies
I like music. I hate exams.

Read the story. Write *a*, *an*, or *the* in each blank. If nothing is needed in a blank, write *X*.

Many families have trouble finding time to spend together. Parents often get 1) ___X___ home from 2) _____ work late, and children often have many after-school activities, such as music or swimming lessons. It is difficult for them to have 3) _____ dinner together as 4) _____ family. The Khan family is an example.

Until recently, the Khan family didn't eat together often. Mr. and Mrs. Khan and their two children – Michael and Sara – were all busy. 5) _____ parents were busy with their schedules at 6) _____ work, and 7) _____ children were busy with their schedules at 8) _____ school and after 9) _____ school. The members of 10) _____ family ate something from 11) _____ refrigerator or they warmed something in 12) _____ microwave. Often they ate 13) _____ fast food*. They used to eat at different times, and they usually didn't have their meals in 14) _____ dining room. Sometimes family members ate in 15) _____ living room in front of 16) _____ television. As a result, they weren't having very healthy meals.

Now the family has tried to change its habits. The family members eat two meals together: The parents fix 17) _____ simple breakfast and 18) _____ big hot meal in the evening. For 19) _____ dinner, they usually have 20) _____ chicken or fish with 21) _____ rice or 22) _____ potatoes. They sometimes have 23) _____ pasta. They always have 24) _____ big salad. And they often have 25) _____ fruit for dessert. Sometimes they get 26) _____ take-out food from 27) _____ restaurant to eat at 28) _____ home. After they eat, the four of them often watch 29) _____ TV or 30) _____ video together. Sometimes, they go to 31) _____ movies, but not on weeknights.

Everyone in 32) _____ family is happier with the decision to spend more time together and to eat 33) _____ better meals.

* fast food: *food that can be cooked easily or that can be sold quickly in restaurants, like hamburgers, etc.*

The . . . (Names of Places)

Answer the questions about the words in parentheses, adding *the* where necessary. If you are not sure of the answer, begin with *I think* . . . .

1. Which has more water? (Mississippi River, Indian Ocean)
   The Indian Ocean has more water than the Mississippi River.

2. Which is bigger? (London Zoo, Grand Canyon National Park)

3. Where are there more people? (Indonesia, United Arab Emirates)

4. Which has more old things? (Museum of Science and Industry in Chicago, Vatican Museums)

5. Which mountains are higher? (Himalayas, Alps)

6. Which has a larger population? (Western Europe, Asia)

7. Which country has more land? (Philippines, Japan)

8. Which is taller? (Washington Monument, Empire State Building)

9. Which is older? (Colosseum, Great Wall of China)

10. Which street in New York is more famous? (Wall Street, Columbus Avenue)

11. In the Northern Hemisphere, where do more cold winds come from? (north, south)

Use your own ideas to write sentences with the words in parentheses. Use the phrases as they are given, with or without *a/an* – do not change them. The verbs can be in any appropriate form.

1. (last month / next week) *I went to the doctor's last month, but I have to go again next week.* OR *I hope it will be warmer next week because it has been cold here since last month.*

2. (the radio / TV) _____

3. (an apple / the orange) _____

4. (an engineer / an hour) _____

5. (a salad / some pizza) _____

6. (a book / the floor / the book) _____

7. (the hotel / a car) _____

8. (go to work / return home) _____

9. (friends / the friends) _____

10. (information / the newspaper) _____

11. (a letter / advice) _____

This/these and *that/those*

A. Match B's responses to A's statements and questions.

A

_c_ 1. Are these your gloves?

___ 2. *(on the phone)* Hello. Is this Tom?

___ 3. The problem is your fault.

___ 4. Is this Mr. North's coat?

___ 5. Excuse me, is this seat taken?

___ 6. Which flowers do you like better?

___ 7. Which watermelon should we buy?

___ 8. Mark got very angry at me yesterday.

___ 9. Cindy, this is my brother, Jim.

___ 10. Who is that man?

B

a. This one looks better than that one.

b. Nice to meet you.

✔ c. No, they aren't. I don't have any.

d. I think these look a little fresher than those.

e. That's unfair. It's not true.

f. I think it's Amy's dad.

g. No, it isn't. He's not at work today.

h. No, it's mine.

i. That's too bad. I'm sorry to hear it.

j. Yes, but there's a free one over there.

B. Complete the teacher's questions and the students' answers. Use the words in parentheses.

Teacher's questions

1. (cap) *Is this your cap?*

2. (keys) *Are these your keys?*

Students' answers

Yes, *it is.*

No, *they aren't.*

EXERCISE CONTINUES ▶ ▶

3. (pencils) _____ Yes, _____ .

_____

4. (lunch) _____ No, _____ .

_____

5. (book) _____ No, _____ .

_____

6. (pictures) _____ Yes, _____ .

_____

Teacher's questions	**Students' answers**

7. (glasses) *Are those your glasses?*   Yes, they _____ .

8. (backpack) *Is that your backpack?*   No, it _____ .

9. (scissors) _____   Yes, _____ .

_____

10. (apple) _____   Yes, _____ .

_____

11. (bottle of water) _____   No, _____ .

_____

12. (soccer shoes) _____   No, _____ .

_____

Complete the conversations with *some*, *any*, or *one/ones* and the words in parentheses. Add any other necessary words. Put the verbs in the correct form.

1. *A:* Are you going to lend money to Jake?

   B: (not / have) No, *I don't have any*   .

2. *A:* Would you like to see a movie tonight?

   B: (there / be / good) Yes, if *there is a good one*   in town.

3. *A:* Should I buy flowers at the store?

   B: (look for / nice, fresh) Yes. _____

4. *A:* Should I get coffee at the store?

   B: (not / need) No, we _____ .

5. *A:* Are these gloves too big?

   B: Yes. (you / have / smaller?) _____

6. *A:* What kinds of restaurants does Paul like?

   B: (eat / in expensive) He only _____ .

7. *A:* We stayed at a nice hotel in Chicago.

   B: (you / stay) Which _____ at?

   A: A hotel downtown – I forget the name.

8. *A:* (we / need / rice?) _____

   B: (have) No, we _____ .

9. *A:* What kind of car are you looking for?

   B: (look for / small / with four doors) We _____

   _____ .

10. *A:* Why is Julia so lonely here?

    B: (not / have / friends) She _____ .

UNITS
78-79

Not + any, no, and none
Not + anybody/anyone/anything, and
nobody, no one, and nothing

A. Rewrite the sentences with no.

1. I don't have any time to waste. *I have no time to waste.*

2. There aren't any new people on the list. _____

3. This store doesn't have any fresh tomatoes. _____

4. There isn't any reason for you to stay home tonight. _____

5. Mr. Ryan doesn't have any patience with his children. _____

6. I didn't have any problems with your car. _____

7. There isn't any milk in the refrigerator. _____

8. There aren't any clouds in the sky today. _____

B. Answer the questions two ways in the negative: (1) with a short answer, and (2) with a complete sentence.

1. Who are you talking to?
   No one.   *I'm not talking to anyone.*

2. What did you buy?
   Nothing.   *I didn't buy anything.*

3. How many cars are there in the driveway?
   None.   *There aren't any cars in the driveway.*

4. What did they say about me?

   _____   _____

5. What are you angry about?

   _____   _____

6. Who are you angry at?

   _____   _____

7. How much money did you spend?

   _____   _____

8. What are you listening to?

   _____   _____

Somebody, anything, nowhere, etc.

Complete the conversations with *somebody*, *anything*, *nowhere*, etc.

1. *Doctor:* Is there __anything_____ wrong with your hearing?

   Patient: No, __nothing_____ at all. Why do you ask?

   Doctor: I just thought there might be _____ wrong because you complained of an earache the last time you were here.

2. *A:* I think there is _____ at the door. Can you check?

   B: *(after a minute)* No, there is _____ . But I think _____ rang the bell next door.

3. *A:* The boss said _____ surprising to me the other day.

   B: Really? Did he say _____ about raises*?

   A: No, it didn't have _____ to do with money. It was about working on the weekend.

   B: You're kidding*! _____ is going to come in to work on the weekend. Doesn't he know that?

4. *A:* Do you live _____ near Tom?

   B: No. Why?

   A: He left _____ at my house yesterday, and I want to return it to him.

   B: It is not very easy for me, but I'll take it to him if you want me to.

5. *A:* Did Roger give you _____ for your birthday?

   B: No. Actually, he never gives _____ to _____ .

6. *A:* Helen said she wasn't going to go _____ for vacation. In the end, she did go _____ .

   B: Really? Where?

   A: To Hawaii. She knows _____ there, so she didn't have to pay _____ for a place to stay.

   B: Good for her.

* raise: *an increase in salary*
* you're kidding: *you're not serious*

Every and all
All, most, some, any, and no/none

Write a sentence with the same meaning as the one given. Use the words in parentheses.

1. All plants need water.
   (every) _Every plant needs water._

2. No one can live without food.
   (all / people / need) _____

3. There are no fresh flowers for sale today.
   (not any) _____

4. None of the secretaries were late this morning.
   (all / on time) _____

5. Some people like to live in the city.
   (some / not / in the country) _____

6. All of my friends have driver's licenses except one or two.
   (most) _____

7. Not all the students in my class study hard.
   (not every) _____

8. All of my cousins live in other states.
   (none / in this state) _____

9. All drivers have to have insurance in this state.
   (every) _____

10. All the people in my office are married.
    (everybody) _____

Every and *all*
All, most, some, any, and *no/none*

Look at the pictures from a picnic. The first shows the beginning of the picnic, and the second shows the end. Answer the questions. Use *all, most, some,* or *none + of them / of it.*

BEFORE   AFTER

1. How many of the apples were eaten? *Some of them were eaten.*

2. How much of the bread is left? *None of it is left.*

3. How much of the chicken is left? _____

4. How much of the salad was eaten? _____

5. How many of the sodas were drunk? _____

6. How much of the iced tea was drunk? _____

7. How much of the watermelon was eaten? _____

8. How many of the plates were used? _____

9. How much of the cake was eaten? _____

All, most, some, any, and *no/none*
Both, either, and *neither*

Look at the information about the four Smith children. Then answer the questions. Use *all, most, none, both, either,* or *neither + of*.

The Smith children	Paul	Sam	Hannah	Amy
Age?	29	23	24	20
Married?	yes	yes	engaged	no
Children?	3	1	no	no
Job?	engineer	salesperson	unemployed computer engineer	student
In school?	no	yes, at night	part-time	yes
Cook?	yes	yes	yes	yes
Exercise?	no	no	yes	yes
City	Chicago (in his own home)	Chicago (in his own apartment)	Chicago (in her own apartment)	Chicago (in a school dormitory*)

1. How many of the Smith children are over 30? _None of them are over 30._

2. Are the boys married? Yes, both _____ .

3. Are the girls married? No, _____ .

4. Do the boys have children? Yes, _____ .

5. How many of them live in Chicago? _____

6. Do any of them live with the parents? No, _____ .

7. Which brother does Amy live with? _____

8. Do all of them have jobs? No. _____ the boys _____ , but _____ the girls does.

9. Which of the children is a lawyer? _____

10. Which sister is a teacher? _____

11. Are any of them in school? Yes, _____ .

12. Do any of them know how to cook? Yes, _____ .

13. Do they exercise? _____ exercise, but _____ _____ does.

* dormitory: *a building at a school where students live*

UNITS
84-85

A lot of, much, and many
A little / a few and little/few

A. Write sentences that make sense with* the first sentence. Use the words in parentheses and *much, many,* or *a lot (of)*. Use verbs in the present.

1. Jason doesn't read very much. (not / have / books) _He doesn't have many books_
   OR _. . . a lot of books._

2. Sue is very thin. (not / eat) _She doesn't eat much._ OR _She doesn't eat a lot._

3. Tina loves movies. (go / to the movies) _____

4. Ahmed is a good father. (give / love / to his children) _____

5. Alice is very busy. (not / have / free time) _____

6. Bill's life is hard. (have / problems) _____

7. They eat out a lot. (not / eat / at home) _____

8. Jerry is very pleasant and funny. (have / friends) _____

B. Complete the sentences. Use *very little, very few, a little,* or *a few*.

1. My car is very reliable. I have _very few_____ problems with it.

2. A: Does your tooth hurt?
   B: Yes, it hurts _a little._____ .

3. Carlos watches TV almost every night. He goes out _____ .

4. A: Do you like your new computer?
   B: Yes, but sometimes I have _____ trouble with it.

5. A: Did you buy anything at the store?
   B: Yes, I bought _____ things.

6. The bus was almost empty. There were _____ people on it this morning.

7. Emily looks almost the same as she did ten years ago. She has changed _____ in the last ten years.

8. Tom's Japanese is almost perfect. He makes _____ mistakes.

* make sense with: *to go together logically; to be reasonable together*

A lot of, much, and *many*
A little / a few and *little/few*

Read the story. Circle the best answer.

Ray's car is getting old. It is always breaking down*. **1)** (A few)/ A little / Few days ago, his car broke down* again. He has spent **2)** a lot of / many / much money fixing the car in the past, and he doesn't want to spend very **3)** a lot / many / much on it anymore. He has very **4)** a little / few / little money right now, so he can't buy another car. So he decided to fix the car himself. After all, there are **5)** a lot / many / much people who fix their own cars to save money. These days there are very **6)** a little / few / little car repairs that are inexpensive.

Ray works part time, so he has **7)** a lot of / many / much free time. He figures the parts for the car won't cost **8)** a lot of / many / few money. He only needs **9)** a few / a little / few parts. Ray will have to borrow the tools he needs from a friend because he doesn't have **10)** few / many / much car tools. If he spends **11)** a little / few / little time on his car every day, maybe an hour or two, he can save **12)** a lot of / many / much money, probably hundreds of dollars.

* break down: *to stop working*

Read the story carefully. Then complete the sentences with one of the words in the box.

anybody / anything / anywhere, etc.	nobody / nothing / nowhere, etc.
one / ones	some / any
somebody / something / somewhere, etc.	this / that / these / those

I admire my friend Ken. He is very good natured. **1)** _Nothing_ bothers him.* **2)** _____ seems very unusual to me because I know he is a very busy person. I guess he is just one of **3)** _____ people who were born happy. I don't know **4)** _____ who does not like Ken. He doesn't say bad things about **5)** _____ , and **6)** _____ has anything bad to say about him. In addition, he doesn't complain about **7)** _____ that happens.

Ken is always ready to help people – he is very thoughtful. If a family member or friend needs to go **8)** _____ , Ken is always ready to give the person a ride. If someone needs **9)** _____ , he tries to help them get it. And he never forgets **10)** _____ 's birthday.

It seems that Ken has **11)** _____ problems in his life, but, of course, he has the same **12)** _____ as other people. But he doesn't spend **13)** _____ time complaining. Instead, he thinks about what he can do to solve the problem. How much time does he spend feeling sorry for himself? **14)** _____ ! He is grateful for everything. **15)** _____ is what makes Ken a special person.

* nothing bothers him: *nothing is a problem for him; nothing worries him*

Use your own ideas to complete the sentences.

1. Most people *are honest* OR *have to work* _____ .
   Most people _____ .

2. Most of the people I know _____
   _____ .

3. Some doctors _____
   _____ .

4. _____ some of the _____
   _____ .

5. No parent should _____
   _____ .

6. None of my _____
   _____ .

7. A lot of people _____
   _____ .

8. _____ both my grandfathers _____
   _____ .

9. All politicians _____
   _____ .

10. All of my neighbors _____
    _____ .

11. _____ , but I didn't like either of them.

12. " _____ ,"
    asked _____ . "Neither," I said.

13. Everyone in my family _____ .

Old, nice, interesting, etc. **(Adjectives)**
Quickly, badly, suddenly, etc. **(Adverbs)**

Adjectives and Adverbs

Complete the sentences, keeping the same meaning.

1. There was a sudden change in the weather.
   The weather _changed suddenly_____.

2. My husband cooks well.
   My husband is a _good cook_____.

3. I'm not going to eat this apple. It has a strange taste.
   I'm not going to eat this apple. It tastes _____.

4. Look at the used car carefully before you buy it.
   Take a _____ look at _____
   before you buy it.

5. Dave is a good worker but slow.
   Dave works _____.

6. My brother was a good student.
   _____ did _____ in school.

7. The judge answered my question clearly and briefly.
   _____ gave a _____
   answer to _____ .

8. The mail is always late on Saturday.
   _____ comes _____.

9. Patrick answered quietly but well.
   Patrick's answer was _____.

10. I don't want to ride with Jenny. She drives recklessly.*
    Jenny is a _____ driver.

11. There was heavy rain yesterday afternoon.
    It rained _____ yesterday afternoon.

   * recklessly: *carelessly*

Old/older and *expensive / more expensive*
Older than . . . and *more expensive than . . .*

Use the words in parentheses to write sentences with *than*.

1. (summer / hot / spring) *Summer is hotter than spring.*

2. (the Pyramids / famous / the Washington Monument) *The Pyramids are more famous than the Washington Monument.*

3. (Mexico City / big / Lima) _____

4. (the Nile River / long / the Amazon) _____

5. (Tokyo / crowded / Nairobi) _____

6. (New York / close to Montreal / to Miami) _____

7. (Iceland / far north / England) _____

8. (Hawaii / has / nice weather / Alaska) _____

9. (Puerto Rico / has / bad rain storms / Egypt) _____

10. (Moscow / has / cold winters / London) _____

11. (Australia / large / New Zealand) _____

12. (the Petronas Towers in Malaysia / tall / the Sears Tower in Chicago) _____

Not as . . . as

Write questions that go with the answers. Use *as . . . as . . . .*

Questions	Answers
1. Do you *read as fast as your brother* _____ ?	No, my brother reads much faster than me.
2. Is France _____ ?	No, Canada is much bigger than France.
3. Has Ted _____ you?	No, I've lived here much longer than Ted.
4. Do you _____ ?	No, my mother gets up much earlier than me.
5. Are apples _____ ?	No, cherries are more expensive than apples.
6. Is baseball _____ ?	No, soccer is much more popular than baseball in the world.
7. Do _____ ?	No, my father works much harder than me.
8. _____	No, the flu is much worse than a cold.
9. _____	No, my brother goes out much more than my sister.
10. _____	No, doctors have more patients than dentists do.

Older than . . . and *more expensive than . . .*
Not as . . . as

Read the story. Then fill each blank with one word.

My friend Frank and I are trying to lose weight because we are heavier **1)** *than*
we were five years ago. Frank weighs a **2)** *little* more than I do – he's 185
pounds, and I'm 180 pounds. I'm the same height **3)** _____ Frank, and we are
almost the **4)** _____ age, 24 and 23. He gets **5)** _____ exercise
than I do, but I don't eat as much **6)** _____ he does. Neither of us is
7) _____ active as we were in high school. We sit **8)** _____ more
than before, and we walk and play sports **9)** _____ than before. The doctor
thinks we eat too many sweet and fattening foods*.

We are both trying to eat **10)** _____ fat, but it seems we like fattening food
more than we do food that's good for us. Frank is a **11)** _____ worse than me
in one way: He often has something sweet for dessert, but I don't eat dessert very often.

* fattening food: *a food that makes people fat when they eat a lot of it*

The oldest and the most expensive

Write sentences with superlatives about the three pets*. Use the words in parentheses. Give your own opinions.

cat

bird

fish

1. (quiet) *The fish is the quietest.* _____

2. (expensive to buy) *The bird is the most expensive to buy.* _____

3. (good swimmer) *The fish is the best swimmer.* _____

4. (noisy) _____

5. (interesting to watch) _____

6. (nice pet) _____

7. (easy to feed) _____

8. (popular pet) _____

9. (pleasant to hold) _____

10. (dangerous for children) _____

11. (pretty) _____

12. (hard to take along on vacation) _____

13. (difficult to take care of) _____

14. (good birthday present for a child) _____

* pets: *animals that people keep at home*

Enough

Complete the conversations. Use *enough* with the words in parentheses. Add *to* or *for* where needed.

1. *A:* What did the doctor say?

   B: She said I don't *get enough sleep* _____ (get / sleep).

2. *A:* What did the doctor say?

   B: He said I don't *eat enough vegetables* _____ (eat / vegetables).

3. *A:* Shall we stop somewhere to eat before the movie?

   B: There isn't *enough time for us to eat* _____ (time / us / eat) before the movie.

4. *A:* Can you help me move this piano?

   B: I don't think I _____ (be / strong / move) the piano.

5. *A:* Did you go swimming in Florida?

   B: No, it wasn't _____ (warm / go swimming).

6. *A:* Ben doesn't play the guitar as well as he used to.

   B: You're right. He doesn't _____ (get / practice).

7. *A:* Could you please set the table for dinner?

   B: I can't. There aren't _____ (clean plates / everyone).

8. *A:* Do those shoes fit?

   B: Not really. They aren't _____ (big / me).

9. *A:* I heard Ben lost his job.

   B: Yes, I don't think he worked _____ (hard).

10. *A:* *(in a car)* We don't have _____ (gas / get) to Portland.

    B: You're right. We'd better stop and buy some.

11. *A:* Do you always bring work home?

    B: No, but I didn't have _____ (time / finish) this work at the office.

12. *A:* Is _____ (the soup / salty / you)?

    B: Yes, it's perfect.

A. Complete the sentences. Use *too*, *too much*, or *too many*. If needed, use *for*, *to*, and any other words.

1. Let's not sit here. (noisy) It *'s too noisy*   .

2. Let's not sit here. (noise) There *'s too much noise*   .

3. None of us did the homework. (difficult / us / do) It *was too difficult for us to do* .

4. I don't want to play tennis now. (hot / play) It _____ .

5. I didn't buy the shoes. (small / me) They _____ .

6. Frank can be very boring. (talk) He _____ .

7. I couldn't see the doctor today. (busy / see me) She _____ .

8. We couldn't drive up the mountain. (snow) There _____ ?

9. I couldn't get tickets to the movie. (people) There _____ .

10. I never buy imported cheese. (cost) It _____ .

B. Complete the sentences with *too*, *too much*, *too many*, or *enough* and any other words that are necessary.

1. I can't use this suitcase. (small) It *is too small*   .

2. Miles is a little lazy. (exercise) He *doesn't exercise enough*   .

3. Arthur and Gwen plan to get married soon. (young / get married) Their families think they are _____ .

4. Rita has trouble sleeping. (coffee) She drinks _____ .

5. Gabriel is four. (little / play soccer) He _____ .

6. Do you need money? (money / your trip) Do you have _____ ?

7. I don't speak Japanese very well. (mistakes) I make _____ .

8. Only six hours a night? (get / sleep) You _____ .

Adjectives and Adverbs

Use your own ideas to write sentences with the words in parentheses. The <u>underlined</u> words are verbs, and sometimes you will need to put them in the correct form.

1. (good / angry / slowly) *If you are angry, it's a good idea to count to ten slowly before speaking.* OR *A good driver doesn't get angry when others drive slowly.*

2. (<u>do</u> / nervous / badly) _____

3. (<u>sound</u> / foreign) _____

4. (quickly / slow) _____

5. (<u>taste</u> / delicious / hot) _____

6. (<u>look</u> / surprised) _____

7. (quiet / well / early) _____

8. (<u>drive</u> / dangerous / carefully) _____

9. (<u>feel</u> / suddenly / tired) _____

10. (<u>look</u> / good / in blue) _____

11. (<u>speak</u> / softly / difficult / understand) _____

REVIEW
Adjectives and Adverbs

Complete the sentences, keeping the same meaning.

Superlative	Than / Not as . . . as
1. Mexico City is the biggest city in North and South America.	<u>Mexico City is bigger than</u> the other cities in North and South America.
2. <u>Ben is the tallest</u> child in his family.	Ben's brothers and sisters aren't as tall as he is.
3. This is _____ _____ I've ever had.	This job is more interesting than other jobs I've had.
4. Mrs. Reese is the busiest person I know.	_____ than any other person I know.
5. _____ _____ in town.	The other restaurants aren't as expensive as The Grill.
6. Mike's is the best barber shop in town.	The other barber shops aren't _____ _____ .
7. The Nile is the longest river in the world.	The Nile is _____ _____ than any other river.
8. Everest is the highest mountain in the world.	No other mountain is _____ _____ .
9. _____ _____ person I know.	Mrs. Johnson is more patient than anyone else I know.
10. Jupiter is the largest planet in the solar system.	_____ _____ any of the other planets.
11. That _____ _____ this year.	Other storms this year weren't as bad as that storm.
12. Eric bought _____ _____ in the store.	Eric's TV was cheaper than all the other TVs in the store.
13. I bought _____ _____ in the store.	My shoes were more expensive than all the other shoes in the store.

Read the story. Then complete the sentences with the correct form of the adjective in parentheses.

A Family Vacation

The Peters family drove to Quebec City from Toronto for a week's vacation last June. They had a long drive, but it wasn't **1)** *as difficult* _____ (difficult) as they expected. They left on a Saturday because they know traffic is often **2)** *worse* _____ (bad) on weekday mornings than on Saturday. They left Toronto **3)** *later* _____ (late) than they planned, but the road was still not **4)** _____ (crowded) as on a weekday. Of course, when you travel with children, you have to stop a little **5)** _____ (often), so they arrived in Quebec late. They went to their hotel, which was in an old building. It was **6)** _____ (expensive) than some of the newer hotels, but the newer ones wouldn't have been **7)** _____ (nice). The Peters thought that it was one of the **8)** _____ (pretty) hotels they had ever stayed in.

Traveling with young children poses problems. The Peters children are only eight and five. Sometimes it can be difficult to eat out with children because they don't like **9)** _____ (many) different kinds of food as adults do. The first night the Peters asked where the **10)** _____ (close) restaurant was because they were too tired to go far. When you don't speak the language, it can be much **11)** _____ (difficult) to order food in a restaurant. However, the Peters found that they were able to manage because most people spoke some English and the children were able to find food that they liked.

The family visited places outside like the zoo, the fort, and the Old City. These places were **12)** _____ (interesting) for the children than museums. People told the Peters that the time of year they were there – early summer – was probably the **13)** _____ (good) time to visit Quebec. People there said the weather was **14)** _____ (warm) than usual for the time of year and it was **15)** _____ (sunny) than normal. The family enjoyed themselves, and they all agreed it was the **16)** _____ (nice) vacation they have ever had.

He speaks English very well. **(Word Order)**
Always/usually/often, etc. **(Word Order)**

Word Order

Put the words in order to make sentences. Some are questions.

1. (at a restaurant / order / I / never / fish)

   I never order fish at a restaurant.

2. (my new car / my sister / very much / doesn't like)

3. (both / work / Mark and Amy / in the same office)

4. (met / him / Samantha / last month / at a party)

5. (at a club / the Wymans / go dancing / every weekend / still)

6. (leave / in the kitchen / dirty dishes / you / do / overnight / ever?)

7. (met / you / have / already / my boss?)

8. (with her friends / on weekends / Clare / time to go out / has / seldom)

9. (still / buy / have to / some stamps / this afternoon / I / at the post office)

10. (the lights / at night / to turn off / you / sometimes / do / forget?)

11. (Fred / at home / eat / doesn't / dinner / after work / usually)

12. (are / both / my two uncles / police officers)

Still, yet, and already

Complete the conversations with *still, already,* or *yet* and the correct form of a verb.

1. *A: (on the phone)* Can I speak to Kathy?

   B: Sorry, she *is still* _____ at work. She hasn't *come* _____
   home *yet* _____ .

2. *A:* I have some news to tell you about Kathy.

   B: If it's about her new job, she has *already told* _____ me.

3. *A:* Do you _____ cards every week?

   B: No, we don't have time to play cards so often.

4. *A:* Here's a copy of my report.

   B: Thanks, but I _____ a copy in my briefcase.

5. *A:* Has the mail carrier _____ ?

   B: No, she doesn't come until the afternoon.

6. *A:* Have you _____ a job _____ ?

   B: No, I haven't found one. I'm _____ .

7. *A:* Have you _____ your parents about your accident
   _____ ?

   B: No, I'm afraid to tell them. It happened in their new car.

8. *A:* Is Angela coming with us to see the movie?

   B: No. She's _____ it.

9. *A: (at a party)* I want to say hello to your parents. Where are they?

   B: They _____ here _____ . But they're on their
   way, and they should be here soon.

10. *A:* We still have to wash the dishes before we go to bed.

    B: No, we don't. I've _____ them.

11. *A:* Have you changed jobs?

    B: No, I'm _____ in my father's store.

Give me that book! Give it to me!

**A. Complete the conversations with a pronoun (*it, me, them, you,* etc.) + *to* or
for followed by another pronoun.**

1. *A:* Would you like more to eat? Some more potatoes?

   B: Yes, would you please pass ___them to me___ ?

2. *A:* Did your sister get your letter?

   B: I suppose so. I sent ___it to her___ last week.

3. *A:* Some friends of mine would like to see your new car.

   B: I could show _____ tomorrow if they're free.

4. *A:* These flowers are beautiful. Who are they for?

   B: For mom. Could you give _____ when she comes home?

5. *A:* Thank you for the gift. These bowls are beautiful. Where did you get them?

   B: I bought _____ on my trip to Japan.

6. *A:* Did you and Jeff buy this sofa when you got married?

   B: No. My parents got _____ .

7. *A:* I like your jacket.

   B: It's not mine. Someone lent _____ .

8. *A:* This juice is for the children.

   B: I'll give _____ .

B. Complete the sentences with the words in parentheses in the correct order.

1. I sent ___my sister a postcard___ (a postcard / my sister).

2. They showed _____ (me / a picture of their baby).

3. I lent _____ (a cup of sugar / my neighbor).

4. They bought _____ (a car / their parents).

5. Could you get _____ (a newspaper / my father) when you go out?

Use your own ideas to write sentences with the words in parentheses. You can change the order of the words given.

1. (forget / never) _My father never forgets to pay his bills._
   OR _I have never forgotten my keys in the car._

2. (buy / me) _My sister bought me a card for my birthday._

3. (be / usually) _____

4. (be / also) _____

5. (wear / still) _____

6. (lend / strangers) _____

7. (photos / show / us) _____

8. (go / rarely) _____

9. (be / yet) _____

10. (learn / already) _____

11. (on the weekend / breakfast / eat / in a restaurant) _____

UNIT
98

At 8 o'clock, on Monday, in April, etc.

Prepositions

A. Complete the sentences with *at, on,* or *in*. If no preposition is necessary, write *X*.

1. Beatrice started her new job _X_____ last Monday. She'll tell us about it
   _on_____ the weekend when she visits.

2. I can't see the dentist _____ this week or _____ next week, but I have
   an appointment _____ three weeks.

3. Aaron likes starting work _____ 5 A.M., but it was hard for him _____
   the beginning.

4. My birthday is _____ next Wednesday, but we're celebrating it _____
   today.

5. I try to exercise _____ every day, usually _____ the morning
   but sometimes _____ night.

**B. Rewrite the second sentence with the words in parentheses. Use *in, on,* or *at*
where necessary.**

1. Today is March 21. My exam is on April 4.
   (next month) _My exam is next month._____

2. Today is March 21. My exam is on April 4.
   (two weeks) _My exam is in two weeks._____

3. It's 2 P.M. I have a coffee break in two hours.
   (4 P.M.) _____

4. I'm busy this afternoon. I'll take you to the bank early tomorrow.
   (the morning) _____

5. I have to study. We have quizzes on Thursdays.
   (every Thursday) _____

6. Hurry, it's 4:50. The bank closes at 5.
   (ten minutes) _____

EXERCISE 113

From . . . to, until, since, and *for*

Complete the sentences, keeping the same meaning. Use the word in parentheses.

1. Alice lived in Brazil from 1992 to 1998.

   (for) Alice *lived in Brazil for six years* .

2. Lily went to bed at midnight.

   (until) Lily *stayed up until midnight* .

3. Les went to the gym early this morning, and he's still there.

   (since) Les has been at _____ .

4. I haven't worked since I moved here six weeks ago.

   (for) I haven't worked _____ .

5. I can take care of your baby, but I have to leave at two.

   (until) I _____ two.

6. Cindy had red hair when she was born, and she still has the same color hair.

   (since) Cindy has had red hair _____ .

7. When Charlie loses ten pounds, he'll stop exercising.

   (until) Charlie will exercise _____ .

8. Sam was an actor in New York for five years. He stopped acting in 2001.

   (from . . . to . . .) Sam was an actor _____ .

9. I worked at the computer all morning. Then I had lunch.

   (until) I worked _____ .

10. Helen moved to Philadelphia when she got married and she says she never wants to move away.

    (since) Helen has lived _____ .

11. Sylvia was married for five years. She got divorced in 2002.

    (from . . . to . . .) Sylvia was _____ .

Before, after, during, and while

Complete the sentences, keeping the same meaning. Use the word in parentheses.

1. Passengers on an airplane have to fasten their seatbelts during takeoff and landing.

   (while) Passengers on an airplane *have to fasten their seatbelts while the airplane* takes off and lands.

2. Bob always checks his briefcase before he leaves for work.

   (before) Bob *always checks his briefcase before* _____ leaving for work.

3. After finishing my exercises, I take a shower.

   (after) _____ I _____ , I take a shower.

4. Mr. Riggan and his brother didn't speak to each other from 1982 to 1996.

   (for) Mr. Riggan and his brother _____ years.

5. Before going to bed, could you lock the doors?

   (before) Could you _____ you _____ ?

6. During the time they were neighbors, Mike and Sally never met.

   (while) _____ , Mike and Sally never met.

7. Students need to concentrate* while they are taking exams.

   (during) Students _____ exams.

8. I worked on the exam from nine to noon without a break.

   (for) I _____ without a break.

9. I always brush my teeth after I eat.

   (after) I _____ eating.

10. Margot got sick during dinner.

    (while) Margot _____ eating dinner.

11. Most people dream while they are asleep, but they may not remember their dreams.

    (during) Most people _____
    the night, but they may not remember their dreams.

    * concentrate: *to keep your attention on something*

In, *at*, and *on* (Places)

Read what the woman in the car is saying to the driver. Complete the sentences with *in*, *at*, or *on*.

"Gloria lives **1)** _on_ this street. She lives **2)** _____ a big white house. I am sure that she doesn't live **3)** _____ the middle of the block. I'm sure she lives **4)** _____ the end of the block. In fact, I think her house is right **5)** _____ the corner. There are some nice bushes and a birdbath **6)** _____ the front yard. The family's last name is **7)** _____ the front door of the house. Gloria and her family live **8)** _____ the first floor. Let's see if anyone is **9)** _____ home. She might be **10)** _____ work, and the children are probably **11)** _____ school. But we can leave a note to say we're sorry her husband is **12)** _____ the hospital. The poor man! He had an accident when he was **13)** _____ his motorcycle. I know because I saw the story **14)** _____ the newspaper this morning. You couldn't miss it – it was right **15)** _____ the top of page one. How did the accident happen? Well, they say a driver **16)** _____ an old car didn't stop **17)** _____ the traffic light. Imagine! That driver should be **18)** _____ jail. What **19)** _____ the world was he thinking?

"Well, you're not talking very much. Let's hurry to Gloria's – I have to be **20)** _____ the doctor's in an hour. Actually, can you drive me there after our visit to Gloria's? My son is **21)** _____ a football game, and I can call him from the doctor's office to pick me up*. We're having dinner **22)** _____ my sister's tonight, and she lives **23)** _____ the next town **24)** _____ a busy street. You can't imagine the noise! Well, I just love talking to you. You're such a good listener. I'm glad we're **25)** _____ your car – it's easier to talk that way."

* pick (someone) up: *to take someone by car from one place to another*

In, at, and *on* (Places)

Complete the questions with prepositions. Then write sentences to answer the questions.

1. Would you rather live __*in*__ a cold country or __*in*__ a warm country?
   __*I'd rather live in a warm country than in a cold country.*__

2. Would you rather live _____ the first floor of a building or _____ the fortieth floor?
   _____

3. Would you rather spend time _____ a concert or _____ the beach?
   _____

4. Would you rather be _____ college or _____ elementary school?
   _____

5. Would you rather work _____ your desk or exercise _____ the gym?
   _____

6. Would you rather sleep _____ a bed or _____ the floor?
   _____

7. Would you rather live _____ a big city, _____ a small town, or _____ the country?
   _____

8. Would you rather take a long trip _____ a train or _____ a car?
   _____

9. Would you rather stay _____ a hotel or _____ a friend's?
   _____

10. In nice weather, would you rather eat _____ the dining room or _____ the balcony?
    _____

11. Would you rather spend free time _____ a park or _____ a museum?
    _____

12. Would you rather swim _____ a pool or _____ the ocean?
    _____

To, *in*, and *at* (Places)

Complete the sentences about the picture. Use the words in parentheses. Use *to*, *in*, and *at* where necessary. Put the verb in an appropriate form.

1. Mrs. Ramos *is at the mall* (be / the mall).

2. She was *at a department store* (be / a department store).

3. She didn't _____ (go / the bank).

4. She _____ (go / home now).

5. When she _____ (get / home), she'll work in her home office.

6. The police officer _____ (arrive / the mall) five minutes ago.

7. He is _____ (sit / his car).

8. The police car _____ (be / the parking lot).

9. The police officer _____ (return / the police station) in an hour.

10. The girl didn't _____ (go / school) today.

11. She _____ (get / the mall) a few minutes ago.

12. She _____ (come / the mall) to meet her friends.

13. Her parents think she _____ (be / school).

14. She might be in trouble when she _____ (get / home).

Next to, between, under, etc.

Look at the picture. Correct the sentences by changing the underlined parts. Use the words in the box, and any other words that you need.

above	below	by	in front of	next to	on the right
across from	between	in back of	in the middle	on the left	under

1. The young man is sitting <u>across from</u> the young woman.

   The young man is sitting next to the young woman.

2. He is holding flowers <u>next to</u> the table.

3. The couple's table is <u>above</u> the window.

4. The big table is <u>on the left.</u>

5. There is a light <u>on</u> the big table.

6. The children are sitting <u>next to</u> each other.

7. There are two small tables <u>on the right.</u>

EXERCISE CONTINUES ▶ ▶

8. There is a mouse <u>on</u> one of the tables.

_____

9. The cook is standing <u>in front of</u> the waiter.

_____

10. The busboy* is <u>between</u> the cook and the waiter.

_____

11. A woman is checking her makeup <u>next to</u> the mirror.

_____

12. The mirror is <u>in</u> the restrooms.

_____ the restrooms.

13. The telephone is <u>in back of</u> the restrooms.

_____

 * busboy: *a person who works in a restaurant and helps waiters doing tasks such as carrying dishes or cleaning tables*

EXERCISE 119

Up, over, through, etc.

These sentences don't make sense*. Rewrite the sentences, correcting the underlined parts.

1. We walked from <u>the restaurant</u> to <u>the gas station</u> to eat lunch.

   We walked from the gas station to the restaurant to eat lunch.

2. I always <u>put</u> the clean dishes <u>in</u> the dishwasher.

   I always take the clean dishes out of the dishwasher.

3. Do you think I should hang this picture <u>below</u> the sofa?

4. Don't <u>take</u> your feet <u>off</u> the sofa. You'll make it dirty.

5. When I walked <u>into</u> the house, I felt a light rain.

6. Don't get <u>in</u> the car here – there's too much traffic. Wait until I park the car.

7. We walked <u>down</u> the hill to the house at the top.

8. Water freezes when the temperature is <u>above</u> zero degrees Celsius.

9. We sat <u>over</u> a big tree and had a picnic.

10. You should turn on your car lights when you drive <u>over</u> a tunnel.

11. If you're warm, why don't you jump <u>out of</u> the pool?

* make sense: *to be reasonable and logical*

EXERCISE CONTINUES ▶ ▶

12. The thief ran <u>into</u> the police station to escape.

_____

13. *(on the phone)* My apartment is on the fifth floor. Be careful when you walk <u>down</u> the stairs.

_____

14. The Smiths are <u>coming from</u> Australia next week. They've never been there before.

_____

15. I had to drive <u>into</u> the hospital four times before I found a parking place.

_____

16. The door is locked. Let's go in the house <u>past</u> the window.

_____

17. You can't get to San Francisco if you don't drive <u>through</u> this bridge.

_____

18. We didn't notice the barber shop even though we walked <u>into</u> it three times.

_____

19. Let's take our shoes off and walk <u>past</u> the beach.

_____

20. <u>Put</u> the dishes <u>in</u> the cabinet. It's time to set the table* for dinner.

_____

* set the table: *to put dishes on the table before a meal*

EXERCISE 120

On, at, by, with, and about

**Complete the sentences with the words in parentheses and *on, at, by, with,
without,* or *about.***

1. My brother can help you. He knows _a lot about computers_ (a lot / computers).

2. This meat is very tough. I can't cut _____ (it / this knife).

3. Mrs. Jordan is old fashioned. She doesn't like _____ (young men / long hair).

4. Do you have any _____ (books / Mark Twain)? I love his stories.

5. I'm sorry you had to come back home. But how could you _____ (leave home / your briefcase)?

6. Do you have _____ (any questions / the lesson)?

7. It's difficult to speak _____ (a foreign language / the phone).

8. The Chinese class is being taught _____ (a new teacher).

9. We will have to open this package _____ (scissors).

10. Our teacher says we must write _____ (our homework / a pen).

11. Is there _____ (anything good / TV)?

12. Is this painting _____ (a famous artist)?

13. Did you hear _____ (the accident / the radio)?

14. _____ (what age) can people drive in your country?

15. Do you go to work _____ (car / or / foot)?

16. Would you like your tea _____ or _____ (sugar)?

17. If you go _____ (bike), you won't get there _____ (time).

Afraid of, good at, etc. (Adjective + Preposition)
At -ing, with -ing, etc. (Preposition + -ing)

Complete the sentences with a word or phrase from the box and the necessary preposition. Change the form of words if necessary.

the accident	big animals	count money all day	do math problems	Gloria
go with us	~~her~~	him	his sister	me
pay bills	people	~~spend money~~	you	

1. Anita is a little unhappy today. Be nice *to her* .

2. You can't go out to most places without *spending money* .

3. We never go to the zoo. My little boy is afraid _____ .

4. Why isn't Sue talking to you? Is she angry _____ ?

5. There's no place to sit in the restaurant. It's full _____ .

6. You know the man I'm talking about. He's married _____ .

7. Please thank your father for the ride home. It was very kind _____ .

8. We're going to drive to Toronto next weekend. Are you interested _____
   _____ ?

9. I'm going to quit my job at the bank. I'm tired _____ .

10. Michelle's brother will surprise you. He looks very different _____ .

11. Poor Tina got a letter from the electric company today because she owes money. She's
    not very good _____ .

12. I'm sorry. I can't help you with the homework. I'm bad _____ .

13. I'm sorry _____ . Did you get hurt?

14. *A:* Is your father angry because of your job?
    B: Yes, he's mad _____ for losing it.

Listen to . . . , look at . . . , etc. (Verb + Preposition)

Complete the description of the conversations. Use the verb in parentheses in the correct form and the correct preposition. Not all sentences need prepositions.

1. *Fiona:* What are you doing with your ear to the door?

    Ben: Shhh. I'm trying to hear what my brother is saying to his girlfriend.

    Ben is *listening to his brother's* _____ conversation. (listen)

2. *Roger:* The tie is beautiful! Thank you so much!

    His grandmother: You're welcome. I'm glad you like it.

    Roger *thanked his grandmother for* _____ the tie. (thank)

3. *Adam:* Have you seen my keys anywhere?

    John: No. Did you look in your car?

    Adam _____ his keys. (look)

4. *Ted:* Will you be here at Christmas?

    Sam: I'm not sure. I might go to Las Vegas.

    Sam _____ to Las Vegas. (think)

5. *Sarah:* Do you want to go to see a movie with me?

    Rosa: Maybe. If it's a movie I like.

    Rosa might go a movie with Sarah, but it _____ the movie. (depend)

6. *Tim:* How's Martin? Is he still in Africa?

    Mary Jo: I have no idea. I haven't heard anything.

    Martin hasn't _____ them. (write)

7. *Alice:* Do you have David's telephone number at work?

    Maria: Yes, I have it in my address book.

    Alice wants _____. (call)

8. *Aunt Hilary:* I'll stay home with the baby so you can go shopping.

    Sylvia: Thanks. I appreciate it.

    Aunt Hilary is going _____ the baby. (take care)

Use your own ideas to write sentences with the words in parentheses. Add necessary prepositions *(in, at, on, from . . . to, until, since, for, before, after, during, or while)*.

1. (5 o'clock / morning / bed)   *Most people are in bed at 5 o'clock in the morning.*
   OR *I was asleep in bed at 5 o'clock this morning.*

2. (married / many years) _____

3. (Friday mornings / the supermarket / my country) _____

4. (the weekend / home / midnight) _____

5. (two weeks / call) _____

6. (be back / Monday) _____

7. (brush / teeth / going to bed) _____

8. (waiting for a friend / study) _____

9. (9 A.M. to 2 P.M.) _____

10. (eat / watch a movie) _____

11. (travel / bicycle) _____

Look at the picture and read the story. Then complete the sentences with the correct prepositions (*next to, under, in back of, up, over, through, on, at, by, with, about, etc.*). **If no preposition is needed, write X.**

FRONT   BACK

A Break-in*

Someone broke into the Martins' house yesterday. They were away **1)** _on_

vacation. I know **2)** _____ it because I talked **3)** _____ Mrs. Kahn,

the Martins' neighbor **4)** _____ the right, yesterday afternoon and she told me the

whole story. The burglar* entered the house **5)** _____ a back window. It seems

he climbed **6)** _____ the fence that goes all the way **7)** _____ the

Martins' backyard. The Kahns and the Garcias, who live **8)** _____ the

Martins, were home but did not hear or see anything. In fact, it seems the Martins always

leave a key **9)** _____ the rug by the back door of the house for the children to

use. But the burglar didn't find that key.

The break-in probably happened about 10 A.M. How do I know that? According to Mrs.

Kahn, a neighbor was walking **10)** _____ the Martins' house at that time, and

* break-in: *entering a house by breaking a window or a door to steal things*
* burglar: *a person who steals things from a house*

EXERCISE CONTINUES ▶ ▶

she saw a car parked **11)** _____ the street **12)** _____ the Martins'
house. A short time later, she saw a man **13)** _____ short hair drive
away in the same car **14)** _____ 50 or 60 miles per hour. She looked
15) _____ the Martins' house, saw that the front door was open, and called
16) _____ the police.

Strangely, nothing was stolen. Evidently, the burglar was interested only **17)** _____
money and jewelry, which he didn't find in the house. He left **18)** _____
taking anything. But he took a lot of things **19)** _____ the cabinets and dressers
while he was looking **20)** _____ things to steal.

The house was a mess. This had never happened **21)** _____ the Martins before, so
of course they were upset when they came home last night. At the same time, they felt lucky
that nothing was stolen. And it was very nice **22)** _____ their neighbors to help
them put the house back in order.

Now the Martins are thinking **23)** _____ getting a dog, which the children
think is a great idea. We are all sorry **24)** _____ the break-in, but you hear
so much **25)** _____ crime these days **26)** _____ the
radio and **27)** _____ TV. I think we all have to be better **28)** _____
taking care **29)** _____ our neighbors and neighborhoods.

EXERCISE 125

Go in, fall off, run away, etc. (Two-Word Verbs)

Complete the story. Use the verbs in the box in the correct form.

come back	come back	come in	drive off	get along	get in	~~get up~~	go on
go away	grow up	keep on	look out	run away	stand up		

Ding dong. Someone was at my door at 7 A.M. on a Saturday morning. I **1)** *got up*
and went to the window and **2)** _____ . There were two police officers at the door.

"Do you mind if we **3)** _____ and ask you a few questions? Your neighbor, Tim
Barnes, has disappeared," the police said. "Maybe he is **4)** _____ from something, or
maybe he has just **5)** _____ for a while. Do you have any idea where he is?"

"No, I have no idea," I said. "Doesn't his wife have an idea where he might be?"

The police **6)** _____ with their story. "The last time his wife saw Tim was a week
ago when he **7)** _____ his car and **8)** _____ without saying
anything. Do you know if Tim and his wife had any problems?" asked one of the police
officers, who looked at his watch.

"I really don't know Tim and his wife very well, officer. But you could ask Tim's family and
friends. Tim **9)** _____ in this town. There are lots of people who know him here."

"We have already talked to his parents. Do you know if Tim had problems with anyone in
the neighborhood?" asked the same police officer, again glancing at his watch.

"No, as far as I know, Tim **10)** _____ with everyone. He is a very friendly guy," I
said. Then the officer who **11)** _____ looking at his watch ended our conversation
suddenly. He said, "Thank you. If you remember anything at all, please give us a call."

"I will. I feel sorry for his family. Do you think he'll **12)** _____ ?" I asked.

"People usually do. If he wasn't in any trouble, he will probably be back soon." Then the
two police officers **13)** _____ and left.

The next day, Tim **14)** _____ home. It seems he and his wife had fought* about
something, and he had left in a moment of anger and didn't tell anyone where he was. They
were both very happy when he returned, however.

  * fought: *past participle of* fight

UNIT
110

Put on your shoes and put your shoes on (Two-Word Verbs)

Complete the conversations. Use the correct form of the two-word verbs in parentheses and *it, him, them,* etc.

1. *A:* Does your father know Vancouver?

   B: No, I'm going to _show him around_____ (show around) tomorrow.

2. *Child:* I don't want to play with these toys anymore.

   Father: Why don't you _____ (put away), and I'll read you a story?

3. *Customer:* These shoes say 47. What size is that in American sizes?

   Salesperson: Size 12, I think. Why don't you _____ (try on)?

4. *A:* What does "sanitarium" mean?

   B: I have no idea. _____ (look up) and tell me.

5. *A:* These library books are due* today.

   B: Yes, I'm going to _____ (take back) after lunch.

6. *A:* Do you still have yesterday's newspaper?

   B: No, I _____ (throw away) this morning.

7. *A:* The children are sleeping.

   B: Yes, let's not _____ (wake up).

8. *A:* Those old buildings are very pretty.

   B: It's a shame the city is going to _____ (tear down) for the new highway.

9. *A:* Thanks for the tools. I'll _____ (bring back) tomorrow.

   B: That's fine.

10. *A:* Does Don still play golf every day?

    B: No, he _____ (give up). He now goes swimming every day.

   * due: *expected to be returned*

UNIT
111

And, but, or, so, and because

**Answer the questions with the words in parentheses and *and, but, or, so,*
or *because*. Use appropriate verb forms.**

1. What did Jeremy do yesterday? (play golf / go shopping at the mall)
   He played golf and went shopping at the mall.

2. What did his sister do? (play golf with him / not go shopping)
   She played golf with him, but she didn't go shopping.

3. Why didn't Jill go shopping with her brother? (not go / not like the mall)
   She didn't go shopping with her brother because she doesn't like the mall.

4. Why did Jeremy go shopping? (go shopping / need new clothes)
   _____

5. What did he do at the mall? (buy new pants / look at shoes)
   _____

6. Why didn't he get new shoes? (not fit / not get any)
   The shoes _____ .

7. Does he have to wear a jacket to work? (can wear a jacket / can wear a shirt and tie)
   _____

8. Why does he need new clothes? (start a new job last week / his old clothes not be very nice)
   _____

9. Does he like his job? (like the work / not know the other people very well yet)
   _____

10. What is his schedule at work? (can work ten hours a day four days a week / can work
    eight hours a day five days a week)
    _____
    _____

11. Does he get a vacation? (be new / not get a vacation for six months)
    _____
    _____

When . . .

Complete the conversations with the words in parentheses. Use any other words that are necessary.

1. *A:* How long has Ann lived here?

   B: She moved here <u>*after she finished college*</u> (after / finish college).

2. *A:* Can I help you with something?

   B: Yes, <u>*before we go out*</u> (before / go out), we have to close all the windows.

3. *A:* How long have you had this car?

   B: We bought it _____ (when / we / have the baby).

4. *A:* Is this package for me?

   B: Yes, it came _____ (while / you / be away).

5. *A:* How long will you stay with your grandfather?

   B: I really can't leave him _____ (until / be better).

6. *A:* Do you have my home address?

   B: Yes. I'll send you a postcard _____ (when / get to Moscow).

7. *A:* Mom, can I drive the car to the store?

   B: Absolutely not. You won't do any driving _____
   _____ (before / get a driver's license).

8. *A:* Should I turn the radio down?

   B: Yes, please. I can't talk on the phone _____
   _____ (while / the radio / play).

9. *A:* Do you want to go to the movies with us?

   B: No, thanks. _____
   _____ (when / be tired), I can't enjoy a movie.

10. *A:* Can you believe Al shaved his head?

    B: I didn't believe it _____ (until / see it).

If we go . . . , If you see . . . , etc.

A. Complete the conversations with the words in parentheses and any others that are necessary. Use the correct form of the verbs.

1. *A:* Why do we have to hurry?

   B: If we don't hurry, <u>we'll miss our plane</u> (miss / our plane).

2. *A:* Are we going on a hike tomorrow?

   B: We can go if <u>the weather is nice</u> (the weather / be / nice).

3. *A:* I feel terrible. Maybe I should stay home from work.

   B: Good idea. You'll feel better if _____
   _____ (stay / in bed).

4. *A:* Can we take a break now? I'm tired.

   B: _____ (not / finish / our work) if we stop now.

5. *A:* Can you help me move next week?

   B: I can help you if _____ (not / have to work).

6. *A:* Do you think Andy will be angry that I can't go to his party?

   B: No. If you explain, _____ (understand).

B. Complete the conversations. Use *when* or *if*.

1. *A:* When is your brother coming to visit?

   B: I don't know yet. <u>I'll tell you when I know</u> (tell you / I know).

2. *A:* What do you think of that used car?

   B: You'll _____ (be sorry / buy that car).

3. *A:* How's the weather today?

   B: Cold. You'll _____
   _____ (be more comfortable / wear a jacket).

4. *A:* Does your daughter drive yet?

   B: Not yet. She _____
   _____ (get a driver's license / be 16).

UNIT
114

If I had . . . , If we went . . . , etc.

Complete the conversations.

1. *A:* You're studying a foreign language, aren't you?

   B: No, I'm not. *If I could study a foreign language* , I'd learn German.

2. *A:* Would you lend me your library card.

   B: Sorry. I *would lend it to you* if I knew where it was.

3. *A:* Is the weather nice?

   B: No. If it _____ , we could go for a walk.

4. *A:* Do you have Tom's address?

   B: Sorry, I don't. I'd give it to you _____ it.

5. *A:* Do you think Ann will pass her driving test?

   B: Probably not, but I think _____ it if she got more practice driving.

6. *A:* Can you play a musical instrument?

   B: No, but I'd be happier with myself _____ .

7. *A:* Can't your daughter drive you to work?

   B: No, she can't. _____ , I wouldn't have to walk.

8. *A:* Do you think our team will win five games this season?

   B: No, but I think _____ more often if we practiced more often together.

9. *A:* Can you take care of my son tomorrow?

   B: No. I'm sorry. I can't. If I weren't working, _____ .

10. *A:* Are you going to the store again?

    B: I have to. _____ if we didn't need milk.

EXERCISE 131

UNITS
113-
114

If we go . . . , If you see . . . , etc.
If I had . . . , If we went . . . , etc.

Check (✔) the sentence that is similar in meaning to the first one.

1. I wouldn't eat that if I were you.

    ✔ a. Don't eat that.

    ___ b. You can eat it, but I don't want to.

    ___ c. You don't need that. I'll eat it.

2. If Josh did his homework, he'd get good grades.

    ___ a. Josh used to get good grades.

    ___ b. Josh always does his homework, and he gets good grades.

    ___ c. Josh doesn't do his homework, and his grades aren't good.

3. Sheila will be sorry if she marries Al.

    ___ a. She won't marry Al.

    ___ b. She shouldn't marry Al.

    ___ c. She is going to marry Al.

4. I wouldn't call you this late if this wasn't important.

    ___ a. I have something important to tell you.

    ___ b. I know you stay up late, so I know you won't mind this call.

    ___ c. It's not very important – I'll call you later.

5. Your mother will be disappointed if you forget her birthday for a second time.

    ___ a. Your mother is going to be disappointed again.

    ___ b. Remember your mother's birthday.

    ___ c. Don't forget your mother's birthday again.

6. If you fail the driving test, you can take it again.

    ___ a. You will have to take the test again.

    ___ b. I don't think you will fail the test.

    ___ c. You might fail the driving test, but you'll have a chance to take it again.

7. If you want these magazines, I won't throw them away.

    ___ a. I want to keep these magazines.

    ___ b. I'm not going to throw the magazines away.

    ___ c. Do you want the magazines? Then I won't throw them away.

8. I wouldn't take these pills if they didn't help me.

    ___ a. I will continue to take the pills because they do me some good.

    ___ b. I won't take the pills anymore because they don't help me.

    ___ c. I have never taken these pills.

9. If Emily weren't sick, she would be at the party.

    ___ a. She wasn't sick, and she was at the party.

    ___ b. She was sick, and she wasn't at the party.

    ___ c. She is sick, and so she isn't at the party.

If we go . . . , If you see . . . , etc.
If I had . . . , If we went . . . , etc.

Use your own ideas to complete these sentences.

1. If I learn English very well, *I will be happy*   .

   If I learn English very well, *my parents will be proud of me*   .

   If I learn English very well, *my boss will give me a better job*   .

   If I learn English very well, _____ .

2. I would go to a lawyer *if I had a legal problem*   .

   I would go to a lawyer _____ .

3. If you spend too much money, _____ .

4. My family would not be happy _____ .

5. I don't mind if people _____ .

6. On my next vacation, I will visit _____ if

   _____ .

7. If there were no money in the world, _____ .

8. Most people would be happier if _____ .

9. My friends will have a party if _____ .

10. If I can, _____ .

11. If I could, _____ .

12. If you are late for class, _____ .

13. It isn't a problem if I _____ .

14. I wouldn't go to the doctor _____ .

15. When it is cloudy, _____ .

A person who . . . and a thing that/which . . . (Relative Clauses)

Make one sentence from two. Put a sentence from the box after the underlined word.

She can speak many languages.	The bird flew in the window.
✔ It is close to my apartment.	It flows through London.
✔ The people have the same first and last names.	They have borders with the United States.
The pen was on my desk.	They are marked fragile*.
He or she helps people with legal problems.	He said he could speak thirteen languages.

1. The <u>service station</u>ʌ repairs cars on Sundays. *The service station which is close to*
   my apartment repairs cars on Sundays. OR *The service station that. . .*

2. There are many <u>people</u>ʌ in the phone book.
   There are many people *who have the same first and last names* in the phone book.

3. Did you take the <u>pen</u>ʌ?
   Did you take the pen _____ ?

4. You should carry the <u>boxes</u>ʌ very carefully.
   _____ very carefully.

5. The <u>bird</u>ʌ was hard to catch.
   _____

6. I have an intelligent <u>friend</u>ʌ.
   _____

7. A lawyer is a <u>professional</u>ʌ.
   _____

8. The <u>man</u>ʌ was a liar.
   _____

9. The <u>river</u>ʌ is called the Thames.
   _____

10. The <u>countries</u>ʌ are Canada and Mexico.
    _____

*fragile: *easily broken; delicate*

UNIT
116

The people we met and *the hotel you stayed at* (Relative Clauses)

Make one sentence from the two sentences in parentheses. Put the second sentence after the underlined word. Do not use *who*, *which*, or *that*.

1. (Do you remember the nice <u>man</u>ˬ? We met the man at the party.)

   Do you remember the nice man we met at the party?

2. (The <u>man</u>ˬwas wearing a gray suit. I'm talking about that man.)

   The man I'm talking about was wearing a gray suit.

3. (He told me about a <u>daughter</u>ˬ. He hasn't seen his daughter for a long time.)

   He told me about _____

   _____ .

4. (His daughter married a <u>doctor</u>ˬ. She met the doctor in a hospital in a village in India.)

   _____

   _____

5. (The <u>village</u>ˬ is in the high mountains. His daughter and her husband live in the village.)

   _____

   _____

6. (They have <u>two children</u>ˬ. The man has seen the children only a few times.)

   _____

   _____

7. (The children go to a <u>school</u>ˬ in New Delhi. They love the school.)

   _____

   _____

8. (The <u>man</u>ˬ is going to visit his daughter and her family soon. We talked to the man at the party.)

   _____

   _____

A person who . . . and *a thing that / which . . .*
The people we met and *the hotel you stayed at* (Relative Clauses)

**Complete the sentences. Use information from the first sentence. Do not use
who, which and *that* if they are not necessary.**

1. Hugh started a new job last week.
   Hugh doesn't like the job *he started last week* .

2. You and Oliver had lunch at a new restaurant last week.
   Oliver, what's the name of the restaurant *where we had lunch last week*
   OR *we had lunch at last week* ?

3. This woman flew around the world a long time ago.
   I can't remember the name of the woman *who flew around the world a long time ago* .

4. Liz works at a high school.
   Liz, what's the name of the high school _____ ?

5. Vanessa bought a lot of groceries this morning.
   Vanessa, where did you put the groceries _____ ?

6. That old building was destroyed last year.
   I miss the old building _____ .

7. We were looking at some photos.
   I don't know where I put the photos _____ .

8. This woman lived next door to us in Tokyo.
   We got a letter from the woman _____ .

9. We waited two hours for a bus.
   The bus _____ never came.

10. I am taking classes this semester.
    The classes _____ meet twice a week.

11. We stayed at a hotel on vacation.
    The hotel _____ had a swimming pool.

Conjunctions and Clauses

Use your own ideas to complete the sentences.

1. If I can't *visit my grandmother today, I'll see her tomorrow for sure* .
   If I can't _____ .

2. If I couldn't _____ .

3. Because I don't _____ .

4. _____ , so they stopped.

5. When the weather is nice, _____ .

6. If the weather is nice, _____ .

7. My family will probably _____ if _____ .

8. My family would never _____ if _____ .

9. _____ a friend who _____ .

10. _____ a person I _____ .

11. _____ something which _____ .

12. _____ something we _____ .

13. _____ , or we won't have any.

14. _____ a city where _____ .

15. _____ the city where _____ .

16. In my free time, I do things which _____ .

17. I don't like places which _____ .

18. I don't like places where _____ .

19. She asked me for my phone number, but _____ .

20. _____ and laughed.

EXERCISE 137

UNITS
*111-
116*

REVIEW
Conjunctions and Clauses

Read the story. Then complete the sentences with the words in parentheses and any other words you need. Put the verbs in the correct form.

One Hundred Years Old

May had her one hundredth birthday yesterday. She lives alone now because her husband is dead. She misses him, but she isn't lonely. She could live with one of her children, but she likes living in her own house. One of her great-grandchildren might move in with her; she likes that idea very much. For May, every day is busy, and every day is new.

She talks about the past, but she also talks about what she wants to do in the future. She is saving money to visit China. Her children want to buy her a ticket, but she won't allow them to. She is a very independent woman.

May is optimistic*. At 100, she has had her share of problems*. Her life has not been easy. But the problems never make her lose hope about life and the future.

May is very sociable*. Although she lives alone, she enjoys being with people: friends, neighbors, children, grandchildren, and great-grandchildren. Every day there are people at her house, and she is always ready to sit down, talk, and eat with them.

May is active. She still takes care of her house and garden. She grows a few vegetables and a lot of beautiful flowers. You can be sure she will be in her garden at seven tomorrow morning unless it rains.

May is a good example for all of us.

1. (husband still alive / not be alone)

    If _May's husband were still alive, she wouldn't be alone_ .

2. (be happy / a great-grandchild move in)

    May will be happy if _a great-grandchild moves in with her_ .

3. (think only about the past a lot / not be so happy)

    If _____ .

* optimistic: *looking at the positive side of things*
* her share of problems: *a number of problems; as many problems as other people*
* sociable: *friendly; liking to be with people*

EXERCISE CONTINUES ▶ ▶

4. (save enough money / go to China)

   When _____ .

5. (not work in the garden / it rain)

   _____ when _____ .

6. (be in her garden at 7 A.M. tomorrow / not rain)

   _____ if _____ .

7. (not be busy and active / not be happy)

   If _____ .

8. (lose hope / not be happy)

   If _____ .

9. (probably not have as many friends / not be so sociable)

   _____ if _____ .